CANADA
CANCELLED
BECAUSE OF
LACK OF
INTEREST

Eric Nicol & Peter Whalley

CANADA CANCELLED BECAUSE OF LACK OF INTEREST

Hurtig Publishers
Edmonton

Hurtig Publishers
10560 105 Street
Edmonton, Alberta

Canadian Cataloguing in Publication Data

Nicol, Eric, 1919-   Canada, cancelled because of lack of
interest

ISBN 0-88830-139-1

   1. Canada—Civilization—Anecdotes,
facetiae, satire, etc.   1. Whalley, Peter,
1921—   II. Title.
FC173.N53   971'.002'07   C77-002103-4
F1021

Printed and bound in Canada
by John Deyell Company

Contents

Acknowledgments

This work is based in part on *The Interim Report of the Royal Commission of Enquiry into THE STATUS OF CANADA,* which was published in 2077 A.D., a few days before Ottawa was sacked by vandals.

The text also owes much to the scholarly treatise *Colony to Nation and Back to Colony,* by Dr. A. R. M. Higher, from which long passages have been reprinted without permission because it is cheaper that way.

"All that is human must retrograde if it do not advance."

Edward Gibbon

"Merde."

Pierre Elliott Trudeau

1/The Botch of a Nation

There are persons alive today who remember Canada as a living nation. Perhaps "living" is too strong a word. But historians agree that the country did exist as recently as the end of the twentieth century and was visited by explorers who are still complaining about the prices.

Authorities discount the theory that Canada was the lost continent of Atlantis. Canada never sank out of sight entirely.

Those Canadians who fled the country before it became extinct have been reluctant to talk about the experience, because they left without paying the paperboy. Many stayed till the last minute in the stubborn belief that Canada was God's country and would therefore increase in market value.

The Canadians were one of the few peoples to become a dead civilization without noticing. It has been possible, however, to piece together what happened to Canada, to determine how the nation that held so much promise took little more than a hundred years to regress to an anarchy of primitive, warring tribes, indistinguishable from other savages except for their preferring a club with a curved blade.

Why bother? the reader may ask. In the decline and fall of the Western World, Canada's period of decadence won only honourable mention. Other countries have shown interest in it for a public service message about the hazards of sitting on a lily.

Yet we cannot totally ignore the national spirit of the country that insisted on having its Dark Ages with fifty percent Canadian content. There may be a lesson for us in the fact that, right to the end, the people of Canada believed the politicians who told them that theirs was a young nation whose future lay ahead. This delusion of the perpetual juvenile caused a variation of Pan-Ameri-

canism—Peter Pan-Americanism—responsible for the popular belief that the Canadians were the first race to succumb to acne.

It is sometimes forgotten that Canada once appeared on most maps of the world. Arab maps included Canada as part of Occupied Palestine only after the Canada Cup hockey series was won by the Tel Aviv Flyers (1993).

Because the map of Canada was divided by broken lines into ten sections (''provinces''), it resembled a butcher's chart of cheaper cuts of the carcass. The fore sections were associated with chuck roast, compared to the sirloin area (Ontario), which came before the stewing beef, Quebec, and those appendages usually used to make soup (Nova Scotia, Prince Edward Island).

Despite this cartographic aspect of joints best kept in the freezer, for a time Canadians were blessed with one of the highest standards of living anywhere. We may find it hard to imagine today, but Canada once ranked second only to the United States in prosperity. Then Canada slipped behind Sweden, after which Japan, France, and the USSR overtook the Canadians in per capita wealth. The final blow came when Canada had to accept free wheat from Bangladesh. One of the most poignant moments in the nation's short history, according to photographic records, was when Canadians received back the fifty thousand pairs of stretch socks they had donated to the Asian Relief Fund twenty years earlier.

What happened? How did this once-affluent nation overcome its natural advantages and backslide into barbarism? Was it because of emotional insecurity as to whether Canada was one of the lesser of the great powers or one of the greater of the minor powers? Did the Canadians, like the Romans, see their religion weakened by Christianity? Were the Canadians their own worst enemy, or did they hire extra help?

As the reader will discover in the pages that follow, the degeneration of Canada was the result of many different factors, accelerated by the rumour that heaven was being rezoned as commercial. Rome required centuries to decline and fall. Canada, in contrast, declined and fell in little more time than it took for its deodorant to quit.

The secret: a diversified portfolio of decadence.

Whereas Rome was dependent on a long succession of cruel, violent, often insane emperors, Canada could draw on all the processes of parliamentary democracy to expedite ruin by several hundred years. Canadians had the special ability to take a fatal flaw and build it into a system of government. Their Achilles was all heel.

Finally, when the northern latitudes of the planet were engulfed by another ice age, Canadians were the last to know.

*Homo
canadiannus
primus*

*Homo
canadiannus
horizontalus*

*Homo
canadiannus
semi-verticalus*

*Homo
canadiannus
colonialus*

*Homo
canadiannus
confederatus*

*Homo
canadiannus
nationalus*

*Homo
canadiannus
depressus*

*Homo
canadiannus
prodigalus*

*Homo
canadiannus
crunchus*

*Homo
canadiannus
glacialus*

2/The Iron Turkey

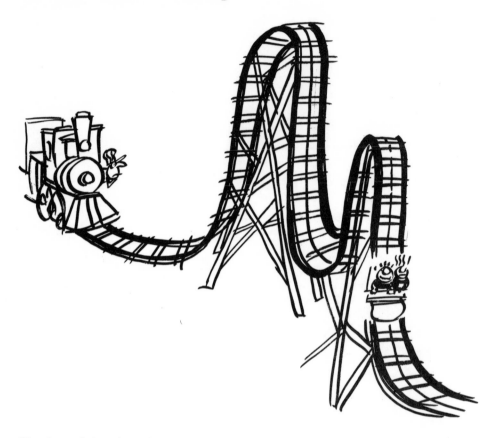

The deconfederation of Canada began with the unbuilding of the transcontinental railway, a feat of engineering rivalling the *Titanic*. For economic reasons, the railways gradually reduced their service, and the oil-consuming diesel locomotives were replaced by coal-fired steam engines before it was realized that Canada had sold all her coal to Japan.

The reason why the railway companies wanted to get rid of their railroads was that trains had become the least profitable part of the railway business, especially trains that carried people. Various innovations intended to discourage passengers—such as scrapping the dining car, while the diners were still in it—proved inconclusive.

The Canadian Pacific, in particular, had to overcome tremendous obstacles to eliminate the passenger train. Because of the precipitous decisions of the Canadian Transport Commission, CP was obliged to hire large work gangs of lawyers—including Chinese lawyers—to find a route through the regulations to the final objective: the converting of the railway into four thousand miles of row housing. This epic task, worthy of the labours of Hercules and given the equally Greek name, Marathon, saw the beating of roundhouses into townhouses. It was punctuated by heroic incidents such as the blocking of the Connaught Tunnel by an avalanche of realtors.

Canadians were so hungry for housing at this period (the late 1970s) that many bought railway property without waiting for removal of the tracks. As a result, they were unable to go to bed in their house without first having their accommodation checked by a sleepingcar conductor.

The passing of the railway passenger train was soon followed by fatal blows to the freight train. The first of these occurred when the federal government took over freight traffic during a nation-wide rail strike, and every boxcar in Canada ended up in Moosonee, Ontario. Before the computer error could be corrected, a livestock train of pigs was rear-ended by cars filled with rice, and the resulting explosion buried Moosonee under twenty feet of pork chow mein.

Even more deadly were the attacks on freight trains by Indians, to enforce their claim to be the legal owners of all of Canada except a body-rub parlour in Victoria. The Indians galloped their horses beside the moving trains, terrorizing the crews by hurling railway depot sandwiches at the caboose. West-coast residents also became nervous about finding poisoned arrows in their boxes of Cheerios. In 1981, a war party of Blackfoot derailed a Canadian National Railways shipment of bathroom tissue—the incident notable because the T.P. was lost on the prairie but it was Ontario that was declared a disaster area.

Attempts to discourage the Indian raids by posting guards (armed with rotten vegetables) on the trains failed because of a union jurisdictional dispute between the Teamsters and the Canadian Food and Allied Workers. Indians also gave the trainmen whisky during the shunting season, with the result that many couplings were sterile.

A news agency (Tass) report describes the sad end of Canada's romance of the railroad:

> **Montreal**   *The last Canadian Pacific transcontinental train from Vancouver arrived today, 18 hours late. It was met by a small group of Montreal restaurateurs interested in buying the railway coaches for conversion into novelty diners.*
>
> *The train carried no passengers, being a freight train consisting of two tank cars of rapeseed oil. The locomotive bore a black wreath above the cowcatcher, and the engineer appeared to have been drinking, since he failed to apply the brakes and the locomotive ploughed into a waiting queue of Yellow Pedicabs.*
>
> *The train was officially greeted by the mayor of Montreal, who declared the trip to be a waste of time because Montreal was now self-sufficient in respect to rape. "If we need any more rape we shall get it from Quebec," he said, in French, and pointedly flushed the toilet while the train was standing in the station.*

The confidence in rapeseed as a substitute for fossil fuels proved to be misplaced. For example, Canadian commercial jetliners using rape for fuel found that it attracted large swarms of grasshoppers. The grasshoppers were ingested into the jet engines, whose exhaust spat tons of tobacco juice. This violated the environment, and, perhaps more important, the planes crashed.

Here Canada's enormous breadth again worked against her survival. Smaller countries were able to power their national airlines by developing an extraordinarily large rubber band. Air Canada spent many millions adapting

You and your "just one more turn . . ."

the European rubber band for longer distances and did succeed in producing a plane that made the Toronto-Vancouver flight in four hours, but unfortunately it took six months to wind up the rubber band.

The demise of the Canadian airlines so soon after the railways proved a crushing blow to the assembly of persons from various parts of Canada, in particular those bound for Canada's most important national institution—the Grey Cup Game. It also made it much harder for relatives to get together for Christmas. This was a shot in the arm for Christmas, but it wiped out one of the few reasons why Canadians visited other parts of the country.

As petroleum supplies dried up further, bus and automobile travel across Canada dwindled to a stop. Very few Canadians could afford to drive the alternative, the electric auto. The electric auto cost $2500, but the batteries were $60,000 each. Other nations were able to modify their automobile industry to alternative sources of energy such as the atom and the sun. Sweden developed a Volvo that ran on sewage. The Canadian-built Volvo proved less efficient on

Canadian sewage, because Canadians couldn't get the lead out. The engine finally had to be abandoned when the shit hit the fan.

Belatedly, Canada tried to create her own automobile in the Maritimes. Called the Buckling, it was a gull-winged car designed to run on fish. The first model, the Buckling Cod, was plagued with engineering problems. The test models functioned satisfactorily on regular grade cod, but after a year or two the car developed an ungovernable urge to return to the sea to spawn. The sight of schools of Bucklings driving off the ends of jetties discouraged the manufacturer, as did the fact that recalling the defective model was severely complicated by the need for divers to locate the car owners in varying depths of ocean.

By the year 2000, most Canadians were reduced to riding either the bicycle or the horse. In smaller countries (in Holland and Britain for example), these means of transportation were not altogether impractical, as their politicians were able to pedal to parliament, whereas Canada's MPs, after the first five or six hundred miles, often lost interest in public life. There developed a lamentable trend to elect members for the thickness of their calves.

Several mule-drawn wagon trains set out from the western prairies, bound for Toronto and the riches that were said to be found there, but the covered wagons were roofed with vinyl that absorbed the heat of the sun, baking the overlanders in their skins.

The plight of the Royal Canadian Mounted Police was particularly pathetic.

22

Having given up their horses for prowl cars, the attempt by the RCMP to return to horseback was fraught with problems, such as attaching a red flasher to the saddle, starting the horse by inserting a key into its ear, and the like.

The grimmest upshot of being remounted occurred when a contingent of RCMP galloped off into the wilds in pursuit of a crazed half-breed hunter who had killed a bartender for laughing at him when he said he was setting up radar traps to snare a fast buck. The entire force of Mounties was wiped out when their horses insisted on performing the Musical Ride while fording the North Saskatchewan during a blizzard. A ten-piece brass band went down with the troop.

Subsequently policemen, like most other Canadians, were obliged to proceed on foot, a means of transportation that severely tested both their sled dogs and their Hush Puppies. "Walking" (as it was called) became mandatory after the Arab nations declared that they had only enough oil for their own needs, which included blacktopping Europe.

By this time the Arab states were well on their way to dominating not merely the world's wealth but also global politics. Saudi Arabia was known as the world's largest executive sandbox. The Bedouins followed their flocks in fleets of Rolls Royces, and Canada was a source of cheap labour for Arab shepherds wanting someone to milk the goats.

Much as Canadians regretted having squandered their own oil resources on frivolous activities, such as heating the Senate, they had no choice but to resurrect the method of transport of their forebears: the waterways of Canada.

Across Canada by Canoe

The last Canadian to attempt to cross Canada by land (that is, water) was Sir Alexander MacKook (later Alexander MacKook). A middle-aged Scot in the employ of the Hudson's Bay Company—the men's socks department actually—MacKook was assigned the task of carrying the Accounts Payable from the company's west-coast store to Winnipeg, where the Bay had built a giant computer that billed customers and determined the best places to put pins in pajamas where the purchaser wouldn't find them till too late.

Borrowing a large cedar canoe from the Indians of Bella Coola, while the Indians were in Bella Bella, and with Alexander MacLuckout as his second in command, and accompanied by two Indian guides, Alexander MacThunderbird and Alexander MacMac, MacKook proceeded up the river. He noted in his diary:

"May 3. Slow progress. After three days of heavy paddling against the current, we find that we have forgotten to untie rope holding canoe to dock. Am already doubtful about quality of Indian guides.

"May 8. Encountering difficulty as the river passes through a provincial park. Water dangerously congested by pollution. Canoe forced to squeeze between steep banks of old auto tires. Paddles fouled by rusty bedsprings. Indians insist on fishing for empty beer bottles, claiming aboriginal rights. Delay maddening. MacLuckout becoming edgy, wasting ammunition on coveys of dixie cups.

"May 24. Several frightening confrontations with wild animals, not normally man-eaters but made hostile by being shot with tranquilizer darts by Wildlife Society. MacThunderbird badly bitten by a banded duck.

"June 12. First experience with rapids. Made five miles this morning, lost twenty miles this afternoon. Should we travel only in the A.M.?

"June 15. Hard to find water to drink, despite great deal of river both outside and inside canoe. Everywhere we see signs: Water Not Potable. MacLuckout and I obliged to accept firewater from our Indian guides.

"August 20. MacLuckout and I now doing the paddling, while Indian guides listen to radio. Hard rock driving me crazy. Would never have hired

24

these Indians if I had known that their sense of direction depended on eye-in-the-sky traffic reports. . ."

Alexander MacKook's diary becomes illegible after this entry. It is known, however, that the party of voyageurs reached the Fraser, portaging many miles to a lake only to be swept over the spillway of an abandoned B.C. Hydro dam. The force of the descent carried MacKook back to Bella Coola, where he decided to spend the winter patching the canoe because the Indians featured live entertainment.

In the spring, MacKook again loaded the canoe with provisions, hired new Indian guides, gazed up the river towards the Great Unknown, unloaded the provisions, and inscribed on a large rock the words: "Alexander MacKook, on crossing Canada by land—to hell with it."

Thus ended the last attempt to journey across Canada other than by way of the United States, where it was also easier to find a motel with a heated pool. For a time the Hudson's Bay Company used coureurs de bois (wooden runners) to deliver its monthly statements, but this too petered out when the trails became overgrown with house plants abandoned by their owners because they were becoming involved (see Chapter 8, "Canada's Change of Sex").

Transportation

Mackenzie Valley Pipeline

Remembrance Day

3/Towards the Prestige Cave

As early as 1977, the single-family dwelling was being phased out as the typical Canadian residence. For some reason that baffles scholars, in that country of vast, unoccupied spaces, land became too expensive to build a house on. The most accepted theory for this strange concentration of people in a few places is that they were possessed by a weird cult that compelled them to live near a temple of a Celtic god named McDonald. The vaguely Byzantine arches of the facade of McDonald's temples were not unknown in other parts of the world, but perhaps because of a patriarchal association with the country's first prime minister, the Big Mac was for Canadians the hub of congested habitation.

Canadians crowded together in urban conglomerates of high-rise apartment buildings and in "townhouses" or "condominiums," which in a few years resembled the row-house tenements of the Old World except that the resident had the privilege of owning his own slum.

The condominium—later called a condo and finally simply a con—was doomed because it depended, like other Canadian apartments, on central heating attached to a faulty furnace. The fault in the furnace was that without oil or gas it lost interest in heating. With a stubbornness born of their investment, some owners of elegant townhouses continued to use their heated swimming pools and saunas after the thermostat had been eaten by ice worms. Most of these Canadians perished in the cause of contemporary living. A relative few were realistic enough to accept their "equestrian centre" as a cool place to hang the horse meat.

It was in this period that Canadians started to kill for a fireplace. They removed the imported French bouclé drapes from the brass decorator rods and savagely beat one another for possession of an open grate, in which they burned their victim's furniture. This unfortunate element of violence in the heating method chosen by the discerning homeowner reflected the failure of Canadians to find alternate sources of thermal energy. Solar heating—successfully adopted in the United States by the turn of the century—was tried by Canadians, and it worked satisfactorily so long as they moved their houses to New Mexico.

Moving a house from Canada to New Mexico proved expensive. New Mexico objected to having its highways clogged with Canadian solar homes edging along on rollers, and it made the owners move their houses back to Canada, a seasonal migration truly awesome in its futility.

38

Research belatedly traced the flaw in solar heating in Canada to a shortage of sunshine. The sun was either too weak or too occasional to sustain a bearable temperature in the house, unless the interior consisted mostly of insulation and the windows and doors were eliminated. The owner then became conditioned to sleeping upside down hanging from the ceiling.

Not all Canadians resorted to solar heating. Some were wealthy enough to pay for electric heating supplied by nuclear power plants, a costly method after the problem of finding a place to bury the radioactive waste made it necessary for Ontario Hydro to buy Newfoundland. This annoyed not only Hydro customers but also the people of Newfoundland, and may have contributed to the breakdown of Canadian unity. The Newfoundlanders were sensitive about the use of the island as a nuclear dump because previously American submarines had secretly dumped radioactive waste not far from a remote Newfoundland fish cannery. The waste had no effect on the Newfoundlanders in the area, but fifteen U.S. sailors who had been near the fish cannery were made sterile.

Because Canada's uranium mines were owned by U.S. corporations, Canadians were obliged to develop atomic energy from peat moss. While safer than other nuclear fuel, peat moss had the disadvantage of having an atom that was fissionable only when mixed with gin. Many Canadians found it cheaper to order a double dry martini. Others tried to burn firewood in open pits hastily dug in the middle of the living room. Their attempts to split wood with an axe resulted in some of the bloodiest scenes in Canada's history, mostly because they tried to use the stereo as a chopping block. More than one died from a severed woofer. Cries of the wounded were amplified by directional speakers, and many a poor wretch spent his last moments being pilloried by a maddened record changer.

The mayhem was aggravated by the confusion caused when the federal energy commission issued a pamphlet entitled "How To Kindle Your Faggot." Barricades were thrown up in gay bars across the country. The National Ballet was refused a theatre because of the fire hazard.

In the rural communities of Canada people were more fortunate, temporarily, because they were able to burn dung. One of the pioneers in the use of dung for heating in Canada was Dr. Ranji Moolu, who combined modern technological know-how with the ancient practice of preserving animal ordure for heating.

The result was the Patty Stacker.

Dr. Moolu derived the idea of the Patty Stacker from a device earlier advertised on television as a means of organizing hamburger. Portions were placed in a cylindrical apparatus, each portion separated by a disc of paper, and a plunger pushed forth each patty as it was needed. Besides making cow manure more socially acceptable to Canadians reared on the microwave oven, the Patty Stacker helped to minimize odour.

The Patty Stacker proved short-lived, however, because not every family could afford to keep a steer. Despite the government subsidy, there soon developed a shortage of bull shit. Also, homesteaders were harried by patty poachers, ruthless outlaws ready to kill at the drop of a heap. Bloody confrontations over a cache of meadow muffins gave new meaning to High Noon.

Some Canadian families tried to avoid the need for heating by taking winter holidays, as they had done for decades before the loss of air travel. For westcoast people this meant a winter holiday in Hawaii, which they tried to reach by raft. The journey took as long as six months, usually with some loss of life, but the successful holidayers came home with a winter tan so deep that it created intense envy in those who had got no farther than Nanaimo. After several of the returning parties were speared to death by these hostile natives, as the vacationers tried to land on their home shore, the Canadian custom of holidaying in Hawaii died out, and the organizers of charter funshine tours were lynched with their own leis.

To replace the vacation abroad, Canadians adopted the ancient Indian custom of raiding neighbouring villages, massacring the men and carrying off the women as slaves. This recreation drew criticism from the women's liberation movement, which had remained vigorous even though the Canadian woman no longer shaved her legs unless they were attracting voles. The women demanded that in all tribal raids men and women be massacred and raped equally, without discrimination. This requirement took the joy out of ravaging, so far as the men were concerned, and they went back to biting rocks as a pastime.

Log Cabin Fever

By the early twenty-first century, most Canadians had abandoned their sophisticated but unserviceable housing and returned to the log cabin. Books of instructions for building log cabins had started to appear during the 1970s, when this means of survival first attracted the attention of people—mostly writers of advertising copy—who sensed the end of civilization as they knew it. Happiness was living in a place that had been put together without a single nail. That the place collapsed when they sneezed was irrelevant. They borrowed a popular saying of the time—"People who live in glass houses shouldn't throw parties"—as the credo of the log cabin.

Later, leaders of government attempted to build log cabins as an example to the nation. The politicians were unable to complete these houses because they believed that the way to build a log cabin was from the top down.

One of these party leaders, a former Prime Minister of Canada, was Abraham Edsel—called Dishonest Abe because of the shady circumstances of his wearing false whiskers during the Civil War. Dishonest Abe prided himself on being a pioneer in the Age of Survival, but he built his log cabin in downtown Ottawa because he was afraid of the dark. It was a rude cabin, mostly because of the kind of pictures he put on the walls to cover his clumsy workmanship. In this simple log cabin, Abe Edsel studied his law books by candlelight, hoping to learn enough law to find a way of getting out of paying alimony. Mrs. Edsel had left him because he was infatuated with the wart on his face, which he thought would put him on the five-dollar bill.

After years of self-taught education, Abe took the law exam and flunked it. He at once died of old age, though only thirty-four years old at the time. This Canadian leader thus completed his remarkable transition from the pinnacle of power as prime minister to the humble log cabin that was his last resting place, the roof having fallen in before they could move the body.

Most Canadians, however, were not so fortunate. They lacked the political influence to obtain a building permit for a log cabin with a bar and bottomless waitresses. First, they had to clear the land. This was not easy, when what stood on the land was a six-storey parkade. Men, women, and children sweated and strained to strip the blacktop off the arable soil. They could work only in the heat of summer, when the tar was soft enough to roll up, or in the winter cold, when they could chop it into blocks. Off season they sat between the white lines, praying before the ancient script: Reserved for Dr. O. O. Kildew.

"The post-industrial homesteader," as the rustic was called, had been taught that building his log cabin was the first step to living in harmony with nature. He was therefore disappointed to find the new Canadian pioneers split into two schools of cabin building: those who believed in chinking the log cabin, and those who were anti-chink. The anti-chinkers, being purists, wore the white hats, the chinkers the dirty hats. Their encounters were often violent. The anti-chinkers were uncompromising in their belief that, to be one with nature, the log cabin must be built only of cunningly-fitted logs, "not a nail in the whole house." The chinkers, in contrast, were prepared to use anything to keep the draft out because, as one of their spokesmen put it, "Nature wants my ass."

41

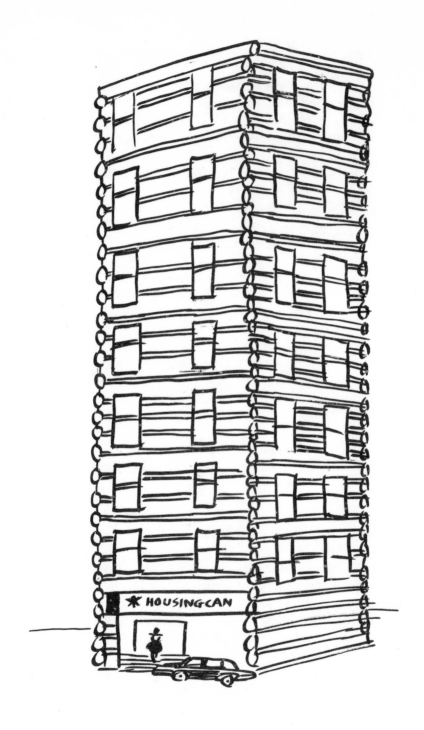

The bitterness of the dispute was only marginally mitigated by the folk songs of the period, such as "Where Are You When We Need You, Maria Chapdelaine?" and the haunting "Heigh-ho, I've Chopped Off My Toe."

The feud between the chinkers and the anti-chinkers became so impassioned that the Central Mortgage and Housing Corporation was obliged to issue a special regulation on chinking, requiring that every log cabin be chinked unless it was already unchinked. However, at this time the credibility of the CMHC had been weakened because its staff was housed in tepees. Although conventional housing starts had fallen off drastically, the CMHC employees still numbered twenty thousand, putting a severe strain on Ottawa's tenting facilities. Space was in fact so limited that the civil servants had to sleep three deep—and that was during the day. At night the overcrowding created real problems in administration.

Perhaps as a result of the weakened authority of the CMHC, the log cabin gave way to the sod hut, a type of dwelling used by early settlers on the prairies who could not afford an architect. The sod house—pictures of which have come to us from the short-lived publication *Canadian Hovels & Gardens*—did not end the strife. A jurisdictional dispute between the carpenters' Union Local 252 and the Association of Turf Farmers led to the Divot War (2058 A.D.). Their dwellings destroyed by marauding bands of sodbusters, Canadians shortly lapsed into the last stage of housing, the cave, where we find them today. (See temporal map, Emergence of Homo Canadiannus.)

Hearth & Home

Renewable Resources

4/The Citizens Band Smoke Signal

It is hard for us to believe today that Canadians at one time communicated by satellites placed in orbit around the earth. Some of these satellites are still up there, waiting for Canada to say something.

This means of communication broke down for the same reason that other electronic media (radio, television) fell silent: fierce disagreement about which official language had precedence. The custom of interrupting the English message with the French translation had already compromised the effectiveness of emergency announcements. For instance, the warning for Hurricane Hildegarde (1983) was still being broadcast by the Canadian Broadcasting Corporation when its transmitter toppled onto the newsroom.

During the late seventies, the federal government tried to appease Quebec by giving French priority over English in such situations as airline pilots' receiving instructions from the control tower. Of the Tower of Babel Mk. II no vestiges remain, but the numerous large craters in the surrounding landscape attest to a lack of fluency in Canada's bilingualism.

The linguistic sickness spread throughout the civil service, whose members had been obliged to take French lessons and had become neurotic because they no longer knew whether to classify themselves as anglophones, francophones, or gramophones. Many of the bureaucrats sank into a stubborn silence, refusing to answer questions in either language. Since they were then assigned to the nation's post offices, communication was further impaired by long queues of people hurling their parcel post at the clerk huddled on a shelf.

A desperate federal government tried to stop the rot by making it mandatory for all public servants to speak both languages at once. To set an example, the Liberal party at its convention of 1993 chose a leader with two heads (Pierre Latete and Peter Latete). A triumph of genetic engineering, Pierre and Peter Latete addressed the convention in faultless French and English, simultaneously, his two mouths finishing their speeches at the same instant. Tumultuous acclaim was his. The delegates stood and cheered as his wife maintained the cultural balance by throwing an arm around each of Latete's necks, and he kissed her on both cheeks at once.

This solution to Canada's bilingual problem proved temporary, however.

54

Latete had been in power as prime minister only a few months before his right head turned leftist, and his left head turned rightist. The conflict inherent in this development became clear the day he rose in the Commons to reply to a question, his right head saying "Oui" and his left head saying "No." Before a stunned House, the two heads then attacked one another with shrill name-calling, including obscenities in both languages and climaxing when the Prime Minister of Canada bit off his own nose, twice.

A lesser cause of confused communication was Canada's tragic experiment with metrification. The fashion of being metrified (a cross between being petrified and mortified) began during the 1970s, when temperatures were changed from Fahrenheit to Celsius, making it difficult for Canadians to know when they had reached freezing point.

People were found frozen to death in snowbanks, wearing Bermuda shorts and sandals, clearly victims of the metric revolution. Those found beside highways were no doubt doubly confused by the change of distance markers from miles to kilometres. Instead of being four thousand miles from coast to coast, Canada became seven thousand kilometres, with the inevitable result that Canadians felt farther apart than ever. British Columbians, who before had merely doubted the existence of Newfoundland, now came to disbelieve in it entirely.

55

When applied to the trackless wastes of the Canadian prairies, metric distances that worked satisfactorily in the relatively tiny countries of Europe caused a kind of madness, a destruction of the will to live, in those who gazed too long upon the dusty highway sign. Such persons often sought relief in the bottle—the litre, which they believed would help them to drink in moderation, as indeed it did, till they found how to get the cork out.

Curiously, in spite of this growing evidence of a breakdown in getting through to one another, Canadians continued to build monuments to telecommunication. The most ostentatious of these was the CN Tower in Toronto. The spindly ziggurat—proudly described as the tallest free-standing structure of its shape in the world—may still be seen today, a ghostly loft smeared with the droppings of thousands of pigeons descended from the carriers used in the last, desperate effort to send and receive messages. (Guides at the site will also show the visitor the cleft stick in which the last birthday telegram was carried by native runner, from Toronto to Hamilton, arriving three days late.)

So far as we can judge from the sketchy records, the only part of the CN Tower that functioned on time was the revolving restaurant at the top, which made a complete turn every twenty-four hours, or twenty-four turns every hour, depending on how the setting sun struck the maitre d'. (Although less majestic than Stonehenge, the Canadian Revolving Restaurant Cult shared with the Druids the describing of circles before the feast.) The CN Tower suffered its final spasm as a despatch centre when one day the revolving restaurant suddenly accelerated, centrifugal force scattering diners over a wide radius of downtown Toronto. While setting a new standard in take-out service, the incident pointed up the tower's failure in other forms of transmission.

Of the millions of messages that Canadians tried to send to one another, only one recording has been preserved with clarity unimpaired: "All our lines are busy. Do not redial. You will get faster service if you hold on. Thank you." This message seems to account for the fact that, of the bodies uncovered during archeological excavation, an unusually high number are holding a telephone to their ear.

The Museum of Anthropology, Nairobi, has a striking tableau of a Canadian locked in mortal combat with a pay phone.

Possibly because the telephone was invented by a Canadian, Canadians never really gave up hope that their call would be answered. For years after the last telephone pole had toppled off its rotted base, people continued to dial, or push buttons, trying to activate the instrument on which, more than any other nation, they had depended to bring them together without getting too close.

The loss of the telephone was especially devastating for Canadian adolescents (often called "teenagers"), to whom the device was an essential part of attaining puberty. While not as painful as the puberty rites of the Sioux, the ritual did require the adolescent to hang upside down for hours at a time on the end of a phone cord. Without the telephone, young Canadians had no way of knowing whether they had reached manhood. From this it may be assumed that the ubiquitous Canadian graffito, "Parents Suck," refers to the thumb.

Young people were not so much affected, however, by the disintegration of Canada's postal system, a means of communication whose death rattle was delivered late. During the early 1900s, the Post Office enjoyed its golden age in Canada, with two deliveries a day in the urban areas and same-day delivery in some cities. By mid-century, this had slipped to same-week delivery and, with the development of new technology, to same-month delivery. Same-year delivery followed introduction of the Canadian postal code, a bizarre jumble of digits and letters which in theory pinpointed any address in the country but which in practice contributed to Canadian Negativism. ("I don't suppose you remember your postal code?" "No, I don't.")

The postal code led to the Postmen's Revolt (1983), during which postmen used Her Majesty's mail boxes as urinals. Known derisively as the Ponytail Express, because of their distinctive hair style, the postmen at this time numbered over one hundred thirty thousand and were more than a match for the Canadian Armed Forces, being able to walk faster, especially up short flights of stairs. The posties also knew how to disarm attacking dogs by throwing registered mail at them. The Canadian government was thus forced to accept a humiliating defeat, and the cabinet minister responsible for the Post Office was obliged to stick a twenty-five cent stamp on his forehead and mail himself to All Other Destinations.

But the ultimate folly of the postal department was yet to come. This was the arrest and imprisonment of Mrs. Daisy McGee, an eighty-six-year-old widow, because she had omitted the postal code on a postcard she mailed to the government to let them know that delivery of her pension cheque had been delayed for eighteen months because of faulty glazing of the window envelope. The jailing of Daisy McGee so enraged the Canadian people against the Post Office Department that they stormed and sacked the federal mucilage plant. For days the streets of Ottawa ran with glue. The carnage might have been less protracted had not the Postmaster General's message of surrender been delivered in error to an Army and Navy store.

The Plague of Logos

During this era one of the most devastating scourges in the communications field was the plague of logos. Logos, a relentless swarm of meaningless symbols, swept across the land, stripping large companies and public corporations of their identity. Like a biblical curse, the logo brought ruin to the written message in Canada.

The logo began innocuously enough on the ranches, in the form of cattle brands such as Ψ (the Fork U Ranch). Although the logo was sometimes exploited by rustlers, changing the Ψ to ⚘ (Tulip Time brand), the confusion was confined to the meat industry. It may have aggravated the cowboy's distrust of communication that involved upper parts of the body, but the general public was not affected till logos began moving, with the dreadful stridulation of public relations departments.

As far as we can determine, the logo was carried into urban areas on the side of railway freight cars. The Canadian National Railway Company, which had already shrunk its title to CNR, permitted its rolling stock to become the host of thousands of **CN**. The **CN** was a rudimentary mutation of the logo. It retained a vestige of the name it represented and was therefore not typical of the completely evolved logo (post-1970), which was characterized by total atrophy of the meaning.

58

It was the Canadian Broadcasting Corporation that developed this new strain of altogether unintelligible logo. Incubated with great care and at a cost of many thousands of dollars—the logo makers were paid enormous sums to create a stylish enigma—the CBC logo consummated a concept: *it meant something to a person only if he already knew what it meant.*

The obfuscating cloud of superlogos quickly enveloped every field of corporate enterprise. All the major Canadian lumber giants began stamping both their logs and their letters with a logo that ingeniously combined the initials of the company name with the outline of a fir tree. Since many of their customers abroad read the logo as the Japanese symbol of fertility, this expedited the total eclipse of Canadian business by the Rising Sun.

Today, cryptanalysts are still trying to decipher the hundreds of minor logos hatched during the twilight years of Canadian society. Like the language of the Maya, the logos of Canada remain one of the fascinating mysteries in human intercourse.

No exact date has been determined as to when these various breakdowns in communication caused Canadians, already a rather taciturn people, to confine themselves to sign language and smoke signals. Compared to that of the plains Indians, the Canadian sign language was of a crude and limited kind. Its most familiar gesture was popularized by a Canadian called "The Eagle," who was the chief of a tribe of lawyers and agents of ice hockey players. Signs involving the use of more than one finger never caught on, nationally, though digital dialects of some complexity have been found in a few regions where self-expression was not inhibited by mitts.

Smoke signals were an equally mixed blessing for Canadians. Because of the prevailing wind, Winnipeg was inarticulate much of the time, and messages read in smoke were often misinterpreted, as when the entire village of Kelowna responded to a forest fire as an invitation to a group-sex party.

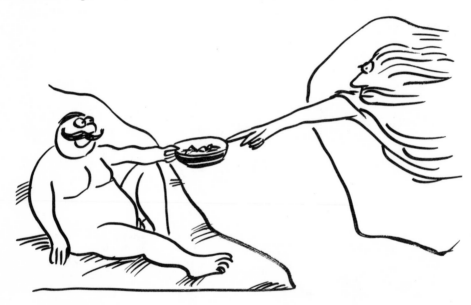

Communications

The Great Corn Flake Celebration, 24th May

La plume
de ma tante
est sur
la table

Conversion to Metric

5/The Fathers of Confrontation

For a time Canada was held together by the populist motto: "We agree to disagree." But soon the various levels of government were unable to reach agreement even on this. The prime minister's celebrated remark—"We have succeeded in synthesizing our severance"—failed to restore confidence in Canada's political unity.

Other nations—Ireland and Germany for example—have suffered partition, but the notable thing about Canada was that it fell apart without outside help. Never was the nation's independence so clearly demonstrated as in the manner of its self-termination. As a British statesman said, after losing Scotland and Wales without a struggle, "We could not have done it, but for the inspiration of Canada."

Certainly the Balkanizing of Europe was not achieved with the same despatch that the Canadian provinces applied to deconfederation. Canada was one united nation as recently as the end of World War II, presumably because most of the people looked upon Ottawa as an improvement on Adolf Hitler. As the memory of post-war prosperity dimmed, however, the force that from the beginning had bonded Canadians together—self-preservation—lost its cohesive power. The people that had found togetherness in burning Washington D.C. in 1814 were only briefly united by burning Ottawa.

Of much deeper concern to Canadians than the threat of external powers was the historical enmity caused by their belief that some provinces were rich provinces (Ontario, Alberta, British Columbia), others were poor provinces (New Brunswick, Quebec, Newfoundland), and the rest were classed as Don't Know.

The only provinces governed by the same party as the party in power in Ottawa were the Don't Knows. Usually this was the Liberal Party (also known as the LP, because it played longer than most people wanted to listen to it). Provincially, the people chose a variety of strange movements called Social Credit, New Democrat, Progressive Conservative, Parti Québecois, and other designations for groups whose political philosophies were never clearly defined beyond the simple, biological urge to form a government.

The growing schism between the federal and provincial governments was sustained by frequent conferences (called ''federal-provincial conferences'') at which the prime minister and the premiers met secretly to consolidate their differences. Without these regularly-scheduled conferences, it would have been more difficult for the ministers to prevent petty quarrels from tainting the traditional sources of discord. One of the oldest and most elaborately choreographed of these federal-provincial meets was a country dance called Patriating the Constitution.

Unlike the Americans, Canadians did not have a constitution that they could bring out on nice days and show to their friends. Canada's constitution had remained in Westminster, in London, apparently because Sir John A. Macdonald did not have room enough in his suitcase for both the constitution and other items that he considered to be more vital to shortening the journey across the Atlantic.

Whereas the United States had achieved her independence from Britain in one bold stroke, Canada two hundred years later was still entwined in Mother's apron strings. This was especially mortifying because Mother had long since discarded the apron for a jumpsuit. Yet the Canadian premiers could not agree

71

on how the constitution should be brought home—patriated, matriated, or (Newfoundland) marinated.

Some wanted to bring it in through Customs, declaring the independence and paying whatever duty was required, while others wanted to smuggle it into Canada as Irish linen. Britain was willing to help, but did not press the matter because the Archivist Royal was unable to find a copy of the Canadian constitution, and there was some fear that it had been used to wrap an order of fish and chips.

The constitution was still living abroad, therefore, when Canada yielded to the internal forces that made her the first nation in modern times to seek colonial status voluntarily. During a period usually associated with the emergent nations of Africa, Canada was the leader of the recessive nations. These were the nations that for one reason or another found freedom too much trouble. Their patriot was the Canadian member of parliament (never identified) who rose in the House of Commons to shout, "Give me liberty or give me a good time!"

The first of the Canadian provinces to revert to a colony was, of course, Quebec. The French-speaking province had earlier proclaimed itself to be a separate state within Canada, independent of everything but the federal baby bonus. When Ottawa cut off the baby bonus, Quebec fired on a Murray's restaurant, destroying several muffins, and the Civil War began.

The Civil War was the Canadians' last big chance to have something in common. The potential was never tapped, however, as the Civil War lasted only two days, the Americans cutting off ammunition from both sides for fear that gun-fire might carry across the border and cause loss of life.

In 1988, Quebec signed a treaty with France whereby Quebec once again became a French colony, in return for which France assumed the municipal debt of the city of Montreal. When France discovered that she had got the worst of the deal, relations with the Quebec colony soured. The colony asked for bride ships, in hopes of bolstering the sagging birth rate, and the French government sent over a barge load of female impersonators. It took the Québecois only a few months to discover the fraud, but when they tried to send back the shipment, the female impersonators took advantage of anti-sexual discrimination laws to demand acceptance as brides. Being obliged to take the brides caused a deep depression among the Quebec colonists, while only slightly improving the birth rate. It helped make them easy prey for the Indians, who gave them firewater in exchange for the skins produced by Montreal garment workers.

While Quebec was reverting to wilderness under a succession of alcoholic French governors who arrived from the homeland with no instructions other than to shoot anyone who shouted "Vive le Québec libre!" the province of Ontario had become even more critically fragmented. The secession of Toronto from Canada, to become a city state modelled on the instability of medieval Florence, was the direct result of the large influx of Italians into Toronto during the mid-twentieth century.

Alonzo the Magnificent

The architect who transformed Toronto into an Italian city state was the owner of a chain of pizza parlors, Alonzo Perfavore, more commonly known as Alonzo the Magnificent.

After he was elected alderman for the Italian district of Downsview, Alonzo seized power during a late-night sitting of the Toronto city council by having his pizzeria send in dinners of poisoned pepperoni. The other members of the council had barely stopped twitching when Alonzo proclaimed himself Prince of Toronto and hired an artist to paint the ceiling of the City Hall. (This monumental mural, depicting the creation of a Chicken Cacciatore with salad, is still visible amid the ruins of Toronto.)

Alonzo tried to establish diplomatic relations with Italy, but the Italian government was out when he called. He then sent an envoy to the Vatican, with the proposal that he would make Toronto part of the Holy Roman Empire in return for the Pope's personal blessing on the House of Alonzo Pizza. The Pope, who was slightly deaf, thought that the envoy was talking about Torino, the northern Italian city where the Fiat Motor Company was making automobiles that ran on pasta. He therefore blessed the envoy's rented car and sent him back to Toronto, which the envoy never reached because his Fiat was blessed enough to cross only half the Atlantic.

These events so enraged Alonzo the Magnificent that he ordered a wall be built around Toronto. Alonzo's Wall took some twenty years to complete, employing thirty thousand slaves recruited from the Orangemen's Parade. When at last the great wall ringed Metropolitan Toronto, Alonzo waited for someone to try to enter the city, but nobody came. The only people who knocked at the gates of Toronto were travellers asking directions to Buffalo. Heart-broken, Alonzo died. The dynasty of relatives running his pizza palaces fell to quarreling among themselves, the feud culminating tragically in the Massacre of the Mozzarella, in which hundreds were clubbed to death with cheese sticks.

This civil strife sealed the fate of Toronto, the final blow coming when the surviving pizzatoria were cut off from supplies of anchovies. This attrition resulted from a siege laid to Toronto by surrounding regions of Ontario, which had raised the Union Jack and sworn loyalty to England's King Charles III despite several letters from Charles begging them to swear loyalty to someone else.

The separation of the two senior provinces from Canada led to the historic meeting of the Fathers of Confrontation. The name most associated with this watershed in Canadian history was Donald A. Macjohn, the Tory leader who stirred the populace with the statement, "The union of Canadian provinces is contra-indicated."

On July 1, 2067, representatives of the Canadian colonies met in Charlottetown, Prince Edward Island, to work out the formal terms of dissolution. After several months of all-night sessions, the party moved to Quebec City because the French wines were cheaper there. The final conference was held at the Westminster Odeon Hotel in London, England, but by this time most of the delegates had forgotten why they were meeting. It was Macjohn who sobered up long enough to issue the proclamation of Canadian deconfederation. The occasion was caught in a memorable photograph, not unlike that of the men who fashioned confederation, except that more of the delegates were under the table.

The first province to take advantage of Canadian disunion was British Columbia. British Columbia agreed to be split from Canada provided that the Ottawa government tore up the railway tracks that were the last reminder of the transcontinental. The west-coasters needed the road-bed for their ox carts, which they used to haul logs and coal to Japanese freighters. Completion of the track removal was celebrated with the arrival in Vancouver of the first mule train. The festive element of the occasion was marred when one of the mules misbehaved on Granville Mall, and several Vancouver residents were trampled to death in the rush to salvage the windfall. (See Chapter 3, the Patty Stacker.)

By this time, ownership of B.C. industries by Japanese industrial corporations was complete enough to facilitate the accession of British Columbia as a colony of Japan—Shitishi Koruma. With the inclusion of Vancouver Island in the Japanese archipelago, the capital city, Victoria, was renamed Fuktyuro. Partial destruction of the city resulted from the short-lived rebellion by retired

British military officers against being colonized by Japan. Particularly bloody was the Japanese Tea Ceremony Incident, caused when doughty residents of Oak Bay refused to remove their shoes before surrendering to the small teacup. The Japanese finally put down opposition by threatening to use defoliant on the Empress Hotel.

Quite different from the loss of British Columbia was the deconfederation of the eastern maritime provinces—Nova Scotia, New Brunswick, Prince Edward Island, and Newfoundland. These could find no country that would accept them as colonies. Although they placed ads in the newspapers of various African states, describing the beauty of Labrador in springtime, no foreign power showed interest till the Maritimes changed their name to Vinland, put horns on their hats, and offered themselves to Norway as an inexhaustible source of sardines.

Newfoundland alone objected to becoming a Norwegian protectorate, fearing that Norse would corrupt the purity of the language. The island eventually declared itself a sovereign state, under a ruler chosen for his ability to spit into the wind without regretting it.

The last Canadian provinces to defect from the union were the prairies. Alberta had already joined the organization of Arab oil-producing nations, to become known as Al-bertah. This official designation of the former province as a sheikdom not only completed the divorce but also gave Edmonton a brief period of glory as the mecca of belly dancers. Salome Upchuk captivated Islam for a time, till it was discovered that the gem in her navel came from Ed Mirvish's. The traditionally conservative government of Al-bertah became even more so with the adoption of Arab customs such as cutting off the hand of a thief and stoning to death a daughter who got herself into trouble. (The latter custom created the Calgary stone shortage of 2071.)

Somewhat different severities accompanied the social effects of the union of Saskatchewan and Manitoba with the USSR. The least of these was the change of the Saskatchewan city's name to Moose Cow. The large prairie population of Ukrainian extraction had been led to believe that the people would share their folk dances with their new masters, as indeed they did, notably the famous squatting dance, with added meaning to kicking themselves in the butt.

What disturbed the inhabitants of Saskobistan—as the new Soviet republic was called—was that the commissariat of food production in Moscow ordered the farmers to plant their fields in wild grasses, as the motherland already had enough wheat. The wild grasses were to feed the reconstituted herds of buffalo, as part of a five-year plan for Saskobistan to corner the world market for buffalo steaks. The program collapsed after it was found that buffalo did not fit into a grain elevator. The prairies became overrun by millions of buffalo and were generally avoided by travellers because the area didn't smell very good.

This disintegration of the Canadian provinces did not immediately affect the federal government, because Ottawa had become accustomed to government without reference to the people. "We have at last freed ourselves from the tyranny of an electorate," said a federal government spokesman. The atrophy of parliament, which began under Pierre Elliott Trudeau, became complete under his son, Justin the Terrible. The prime minister had for some time been

The National Dream

ignoring the House of Commons unless he needed a quiet place to go jogging.
When, to protest their sense of futility, a group of MPs threatened to join hands
and jump into the Ottawa River, the prime minister tried to mollify them by
loaning them his scuba gear.

Ottawa had anticipated the loss of the provinces and the reduction of Canada's population from twenty-three million to two hundred and thirty thousand
by renaming itself the National Capital Region. This made everyone a civil ser-
vant and was, in a way, the realization of the Canadian Dream. To replace the
tax funds that vanished with disunion, Revenue Canada sent tax collectors into
the surrounding countryside, to acquaint the villagers with a simplified T4 tax
return that gave the taxpayer the option of giving everything to the government
or having his house burned down.

To discourage enquiries from the villagers as to what became of their tax
dollars, the National Capital Region directed its beautification program
towards turning the Rideau Canal into the world's longest moat. Indeed the National Capital Region might still be standing today, had the architects not forgotten that the moat would freeze over in winter.

Confederation

The day they brought back the Constitution

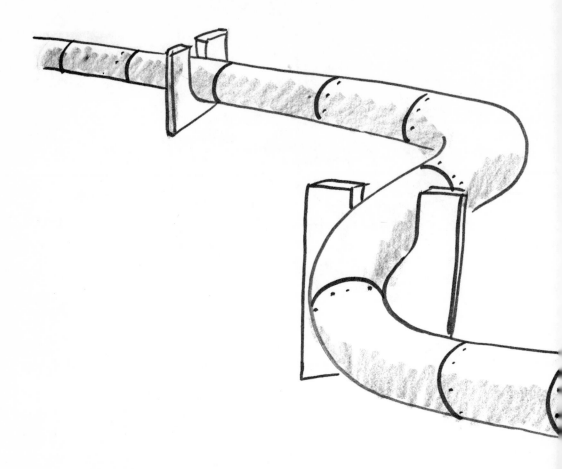

Mackenzie Pipeline

Département
d'intégration
culturelle

Mon pays c'est l'hiver

6/Crumbs in the Breadbasket

Agriculture was known to Canadians. They sometimes pretended not to know it if they met it in town, but the fact was that at one time the country was known as "the breadbasket of the Empire." This was a reference to Canada's capacity to produce so much wheat that Britain had to colonize much of Africa and Asia to avoid being buried under flour.

Canada also shipped abroad enormous quantities of lumber, harvested from her endless forests, and fish, taken from her teeming seas, and minerals, stripped from her bountiful rock. No other people has had to develop poverty in the midst of such abundance. That Canadians were able to overcome these blessings and turn the land of plenty into the land of unemployment insurance is one of the classic triumphs of human perversity.

They began the work on the prairies, with the fateful tractor. In Canada the star-crossed romance of Romeo-Juliet was relived as Massey-Harris. The machine reduced the number of farmers and farms, till by 1989 all the grain was being grown by one farmer—Cyrus O. Gross, of Mossbank, Saskatchewan. Gross sat all day at the push-button console that controlled thousands of unmanned, radio-controlled tractors, spreaders and combines. While more economical than the small farm, his operation was not without its hazards, as was shown when Gross had to go to the bathroom unexpectedly and some of his automated equipment ploughed under the town of Brandon.

In 1991, Farmer Gross had a record yield of two billion bushels, and he applied for social welfare. The reason why he had to go on the relief roll was that Russia and China had a good crop of grain. For decades the Canadian farmer had depended on poor crops in Asia for sale of Canadian wheat. A severe drought in the USSR was a new dishwasher in Saskatoon. Hailstones in Mongolia were pennies from heaven to Medicine Hat. But when the skies smiled upon Asia, the Canadian farmer demanded compensation from the government for an Act of God. Thus it was that a series of bumper harvests in other parts of the world spelled ruin for Cyrus Gross. His computerized grain elevators overflowed, blocking the main streets of dozens of prairie towns and feeding a tidal wave of gophers that engulfed Regina and swept into the legislative building even as the MLAs inside argued about the wording of a telegram to the Canadian Wheat Marketing Board.

More catastrophic still was the great Canadian egg glut. The medical belief of the time held that eating one egg a week could be harmful to the health of the unborn chicken. It was also thought that eating more than one egg a week could give the human being heart disease and cause his toes to turn yellow and wrinkly. Yet Canadian poultrymen continued to encourage their hens to lay more eggs. They did this by leaving the lights on in the poultry shed twenty-four hours a day, which fooled the hens into thinking that they were working on commission.

The poultrymen sold their eggs to the Egg Marketing Board, one of several marketing boards set up by the Canadian government to subsidize increased production of farm products of which there was an over-supply, and to buy them from the producer at a price higher than anyone would have paid for them if he had wanted them, which he didn't.

Of these marketing boards, none was more feared than the Egg Marketing Board. The Egg Marketing Board bought up surplus Canadian eggs with a ruthlessness that earned it the nickname Attila the Hen. Even the Tobacco Marketing Board, which continued to subsidize the Canadian tobacco grower after the government had banned tobacco as a deadly poison, quailed before the awesome power of the Egg Marketing Board. When other marketing boards—for powdered milk, or for applesauce—tried to find places to store their redundant products, they found them already full of eggs.

By 1977, the rise in the power of the Egg Marketing Board was stirring alarm in neighbouring states, such as the United States and Iceland. The board had stockpiled fifty billion rotten eggs in various parts of Canada. As an offensive weapon the EMB was estimated by military experts to have a destructive force one hundred times greater than the Nagasaki bomb. "A Doomsday weapon" was the description given by *Jane's Fighting Muck,* the definitive review of rubbish as a factor in the balance of terror. It estimated that if all of Canada's rotten eggs were dropped simultaneously, no one would be surprised.

Canada was summoned before the United Nations General Assembly to answer the charge of preparing for a peculiarly inhumane type of warfare. The vote went heavily against her. Canada was forced to dismantle her hens. The rotten eggs, accompanied by an international inspection team, were transported by special train to Ottawa and were buried under the House of Commons, where an accidental leak would not endanger innocent lives.

The Waterbed Affair

Canada's collapse as an industrial nation was equally dramatic because of the Waterbed Affair.

During the twilight years of Canadian hedonism, it was fashionable to own a waterbed, preferably a Danish waterbed, designed for going off the deep end. The waterbed played much the same role among Canadian voluptuaries as did

the Roman baths in the time of Caligula, without the engineering feat of the aqueduct. It has been suggested that the waterbed held a nostalgic appeal for a people whose earliest means of transport was by lake or stream. The cries of discovery emitted by Radisson and Hearne found an echo, it was said, in the gurgle of the upholstered pond.

Whatever the stimulus, by 1985, Canada had become a major exporter of waterbeds. The solid parts of the waterbed were imported—mostly from Japan—and assembled in Canada, the Made In Canada label being valued because Canada had four fifths of the world's fresh water and it gave the customer a feeling of security to know that he was buying a bed he could drink.

The Waterbed Affair was a political scandal that evolved after the Conservative prime minister was implicated in a break-in by "burglars" of an Ottawa hotel where Liberal campaign organizers were testing a waterbed. The Tories hoped to catch the Liberals in the act of forming a Crown corporation that would market a new waterbed called The Hydrofrolic. The Hydrofrolic was the first Canadian waterbed equipped with a vibrator, to simulate sleeping in the Bay of Fundy. The burgling attempt was frustrated, however, when the intruders attempted to take a sample of the waterbed and flooded the hotel lobby.

As a result of the Waterbed Affair, the prime minister was forced to resign, the Conservative party replacing him with a leader whose personal physician swore that he had a bad back and had to sleep on a sheet of Canadian plywood.

This gesture was not enough to sustain Canada's forest industry, however, which was hard hit because houses in other countries were being built more cheaply of compressed seaweed. As the industry became almost entirely dependent on the sale of newsprint, Canada became one of the stoutest champions of a free press throughout the world, not hesitating to bribe any government official in a position to influence a newspaper to enlarge its comics. The Canadian government signed numerous pacts with other countries, having defined its foreign policy as "If it looks good on paper, it will look good anywhere."

The forest industry also sponsored an order of Canadian missionaries to go to the jungles of South America and convert the natives to floral bathroom tissue. The natives, recognizing the floral tissue as a magic to steal their soul from behind, ate the missionaries. Nor did the forest companies have a great deal of success financing medical research to develop a male birth control device made from bark chips. A Boy Scout set fire to himself.

The companies finally went bankrupt paying for TV commercials, which showed that all they did in the woods was plant seedlings and help fawns find their mothers. The government was forced to take over the forest industry, and it was during this period that the crown corporation attempted to introduce the coconut palm to British Columbia. It was hoped that the plantations of coconut palms would encourage Canadians to spend their winter vacations in Canada and perhaps would attract Mexican tourists looking for something different in the way of dysentery.

The government foresters did, in fact, succeed in developing a coconut palm that was resistant to frost, and they planted three thousand square miles in palms before they discovered that the coconut was mating with Okanagan tree fruits to produce a bearded McIntosh and a cherry with a ten pound pip.

This reduced Canadian exports to hard liquor. Canadian rye whisky had carried the name of Canada to every corner of the globe that had a bar, and Canadian brand names found admirers in many a foreign gutter. Italy had its Sistine Chapel, France had the Louvre, but Canada had the name that flashed in largest lights over New York Times Square: Canadian Club. Proof that Canada's greatest contribution to the theatre was made during the intermission.

The reason for this expertise in grain alcohol was that Canadians were not a naturally vivacious people, hence their mastery—often likened to that of the dour Scot—of the art of manufacturing a synthetic substitute for the will to live. In Canada, the whisky was sold only at government liquor stores, in order to impress upon the people that feeling good should not be allowed to conflict with banking hours.

The downfall of the Canadian distilleries began when they sponsored sports events as a method of advertising. Because of the prevalence of alcoholism in Canada, the federal government prohibited the mention of a distiller's name except as the "angel" for a prominent athletic contest—the first exploitation of the liver as a renewable resource since Prometheus.

Canadians drank a certain brand of rye because they believed that professional football was good for the nation. Or they drank a certain brand of beer in order to improve Canadian skiing. Still others smoked a certain brand of cigarette with a view to better tennis. A few Canadians were all-rounders, supporting a wide variety of sports till the arrival of the inhalator van.

This curious state of affairs led to confusion among Canadians over whether they were attending spectator sports so that they could drink, or drinking so that they could attend spectator sports. The extent of the crossed purposes became apparent at a distiller's annual banquet honouring outstanding professional football players, when the Canadian Rookie of the Year award went to a quarterback who set a new record for throwing up.

This dependence of Canada's most vigorous industry upon professional athletes proved to be its undoing. Professional sport waned with the elimination of the competitive element (the players' unions having defined the effort to win as a form of scabbing). The Losers Hall of Fame, built to preserve the memorabilia of Canadian athletes who had made a unique contribution to crushing defeat, never really caught on with the Canadian public, who went back to making dandelion wine.

Secondary industry having succumbed with the primary, Canadians quickly regressed to the role of hewers of wood and drawers of water, though they still expected room service. They never accepted their being a re-underdeveloped nation. They thought it was a lack of Vitamin E.

Growth

7/Chaos (Canada) Inc.

How did Canada come apart? The question has puzzled historians, though not as much as how to get the silver wrapper off Swiss cheese.

To understand the disintegration of Canadian society we must study the trend established during the latter half of the twentieth century, when the one goal that Canadians shared, as a nation, was Early Retirement. They bent their energies to building tax shelters and retirement savings plans that would enable them to grow old while they were still young.

Why, for Canadians, was the main interest in life death benefits? The answer seems to lie with what they called their ''inferiority complex.'' This complex, which by 1948 covered all parts of Canada with a thin layer of emotional insecurity, was caused by being close to the United States. Because there were two hundred million people living right beside twenty million people, it was believed that any Canadian who was more than one tenth as good as an American was being pretentious.

Militarily, Canada stood under the U.S. defence umbrella. Canadians had been standing under the umbrella for so long that they sometimes forgot who was holding it, and they threw cold water on themselves as a reminder that their hands were free but they shouldn't move their feet.

They joined the NATO team as the taxi squad. Canadian troops were popular with the United Nations peacekeeping force because the combatants trusted them to be their own worst enemy. They had a special military capability to take both sides at once, leaving themselves in the middle. This impartiality of the Canadian was legendary. Some even thought that the Canadian army developed a tank that had only one gear: neutral.

Canadians visited Europe in large numbers during the heyday of world travel, because it gave them the chance to be mistaken for Americans. They believed that foreigners liked them better than tourists from the United States. The basis for this delusion is obscure but may have grown out of their observing that Americans travelled abroad with an obtrusive phallic symbol (the cigar), while Canadians wore a maple leaf and were therefore more modest.

When the Vietnam War plucked a tail feather from the American eagle, Canada was quick to seize the quill and write herself a note of congratulation on not becoming involved. With the further moulting of self-confidence in the United States under President Richard Nixon, Canadians enjoyed a brief, euphoric belief that their inferiority was possibly exaggerated. While they never reached the stage of pledging allegiance to the flag, they did give the maple leaf equal time on the flagpole.

Politically, this new Canadian self-confidence took the form of a movement to regain ownership of Canada from American industries. The Committee for an Independent Canada agitated to have the country registered in its own name. The main result of this campaign was that Canada won freedom from parentheses. The brackets were removed from companies such as Shell (Canada) Ltd. and Ford (Canada) Ltd., which became Shell Canada Ltd. and Ford Canada Ltd. In terms of national liberation, the deparenthesization of Canada was probably the least noticeable revolution in the history of mankind. The impression of Canada as something inserted as a formality remained strong enough to temper the rejoicing of the nationalists.

Another outbreak of Canadian nationalism during the 60s was the adoption of a Canadian flag, in the design of the leaf of a deciduous tree. Canadians were the first people to give mystic significance to a tree since the worshippers of the Golden Bough. Just as the ancients attributed divine powers to the mistletoe, as the soul of the oak tree, so did Canadians see magic in the maple. According to Dr. Uri Walla, Professor of Anthropology at the University of Uganda, Canadians identified with the sap of the eastern maple, whose spirit could be caught in a bucket.

Historians have wondered why Canada did not choose, for her flag, a verdant leaf representing new growth. They have concluded that the nation had a strong empathy, politically, with something that was at the mercy of the wind. The Canadian was not a man for all seasons but was attuned to turning scarlet before falling to the ground.

Canadians did rise, reluctantly, for the national anthem, "O Canada," at major spectacles such as football and hockey games. They did not sing the anthem themselves but hired a Canadian tenor to sing it for them. They preferred to exercise patriotism by proxy. Besides, most Canadians were unsure of the words of "O Canada," which existed in several versions in English and French. For example, the words "We stand on guard for thee" were gradually eliminated as being unnecessarily provocative for a country that had no nuclear weapons of her own. The new words—"We stand around for thee"—could be sung without affecting the crowd's chanting *"De-fence!"* at the Canadian football team, which was made up mostly of Americans.

Canada still managed to offend the United States, however, when Saskatchewan nationalized its potash industry. The provincial government thought that because potash was a fertilizer, no one would notice, but the foreign owners of the Canadian potash industry were deeply shocked. Canada had never nationalized anything before. Foreign investors expected that sort of thing from South American countries, but they understood Canadians to be unpossessive, especially of their own property.

The United States, in particular, was gravely disillusioned. The Americans had already become upset with Canada's determination to hold her water. The United States regarded Canadian rivers and lakes as a continental resource, whereas Canadians saw them as a place to go fishing without their wives. They were not prepared to let the Americans take more of their water unless they also took as many wives as were in excess of Canada's future needs.

Relations between the two countries worsened further when Canada showed a proprietary interest in her own oil and natural gas. Because Canada also imported petroleum, she was never sure whether she was a have or a have-not nation, and nobody would tell her. At one point, Canada applied for inclusion in the Third World. The Third World refused her because it would have affected property values. Canada was finally admitted to the Fourth World, along with the Moon, as an area rich in minerals but inimical to life.

The Great Canadian Pipe Dream

To exploit the demand for oil and natural gas, Canadians planned to build a pipeline from the Arctic to a service station on Bloor Street, Toronto. The project was intended to make Canada self-sufficient in gas for twenty-five years, or till the United States took it, whichever came first. The pipeline plan drew objections from environmentalists, who feared permanent damage to the fragile permafrost. This concern for frozen gravel, at a time when the developer's bulldozer was gobbling up prime agricultural land around the cities, may strike us as odd. Were Canadians less responsive to fertility than to the frigid? Certainly the threatened violation of the alluvial plain excited a passion they normally reserved for unsightly hair.

Better documented is the resistance of the native people to the pipeline, the story told by such Eskimo carvings as the priceless Hunter Spearing Oil Company Lawyer and the deeply moving Tanker Crud. The natives made a strong

case against the pipeline's detrimental effect on the herds of caribou that provided them with meat. They believed that when the migrating caribou encountered the pipeline, they would become depressed, having to detour as far south as Pueblo, Arizona. By the time the caribou got back to the Arctic, they would be nothing but skin and antlers. The natives demanded compensation for having to live off coatracks.

Because of these various protests, the Canadian government held a hearing. This was something the Canadians were very good at. Their government could hold a hearing longer than anyone else anywhere. Other people went blue in the face and exploded, trying to hold their hearing for as long a time as the Canadians did. The pipeline hearing gave Canada a chance to prove that it could hold a hearing under ice as well as under water, with the help of a few people from the audience.

The pipeline hearing might indeed have gone on forever—beating the record set by the construction of the Great Wall of China—had not the project run into a technological problem when a polar bear got stuck inside a length of pipe being tested for resistance to ice worms. Because the polar bear was a protected species and could not be shot, and because it ate the president of a U.S. consortium of oil companies who tried to reason with it, the Arctic pipeline hearing was adjourned while someone sent out for more ice.

This disappointed the Canadian Indians of the southern plains, who had been looking forward to the building of the oil pipeline so that they could blow it up.

During this period of Canadian history, the Indians in most parts of the country were claiming legal ownership of all of Canada except Lake Erie, which had died. The Indians began their campaign for repossessing the land by setting up roadblocks and beating their drums in the malls of shopping centres, where the whites were already milling around, dazed by the price of tinned shrimp.

These activities became more militant following the historic decision by the Supreme Court of Canada that all the Indian treaties were invalid because Queen Victoria signed them under the impression that they were laundry lists.

In their successful campaign to take back Canada, the Indians were led by the remarkable chief, Standing Cow. A distant relative of Sitting Bull on his mother's side, Standing Cow coordinated the efforts of the Indian tribes by showing great dignity, by refusing to compromise on the just claims of the Canadian Indian, and by appearing in several American movies that were favourably reviewed by *Time* magazine.

Standing Cow displayed great magnanimity towards the white people of Canada, allowing them to carry on their traditional ways within the bounds of their large reservations. He even encouraged them to keep their own cemeteries, saying, "The only good Caucasian is a dead Caucasian." However, the well-intentioned effort by the Indians to preserve the Canadian white man's distinctive customs, songs, and dances was hindered by the fact that he didn't have any.

Whereas the American Indian Movement (AIM) was characterized by a good deal of bloodshed, the assimilation of the Canadian white man into Indian society was relatively peaceful. Most of the casualties were incurred by whites learning to hunt game with the bow and arrow and falling into rivers while trying to spear salmon.

Standing Cow was patient in dealing with the excessive drinking by the whites on their reservations. In tribal council with other elders, he explained that the white people were still drinking to unwind, though they no longer had anything to get wound up about. To rehabilitate unruly whites, he sent them into the woods to pick berries, in company with professional berry-pickers—bears. He expressed disappointment that few stayed with the course long enough to graduate.

Nationalism

Heritage Day

*March past of the last surviving private
in the Canadian Armed Forces*

*Presentation of an all expense paid, round trip to Hawaii
to the 28,000,000th recipient of the Order of Canada*

8/Canada's Change of Sex

In Canada, sexual excess never plumbed the depths of depravity attained by the Roman orgy, but was largely confined to drive-in movies. Decadent though imperial Rome was, it never tried to engage in group sex in a chariot, and not merely because it would have frightened the horses. Canadians, in contrast, considered venery to be part of their vehicle licence. To the end, they looked upon sex as something to be indulged in while watching the main feature.

There is even some doubt that they bothered to unfasten their seat belts. The University of Nairobi Museum of Anthropology has a plaster cast of a fossilized Canadian couple caught by a mudslide in the act of making love. Both are holding large boxes of popcorn.

Some scholars have explained this peculiar attitude—that is, treating sexual intercourse as a subsidiary entertainment—as part of the nation's heritage from the British, who ''took their pleasures sadly'' till World War II introduced them to the opportunities of the bomb shelter. Others ascribe Canada's failure to pioneer new frontiers of ''fooling around'' (as it was called) to the early respect for women as something scarce. Until well into the twenty-first century, men outnumbered women in Canada, without learning how to take advantage of it. The only place in Canada where the female population exceeded the male was Ottawa. Canadian men were therefore conditioned to think of women as either virgins or civil servants, unable to respond sexually without having three references from the applicant's doctor, minister, bank manager, or notary public.

In the early days, the women with whom men felt comfortable were the dancehall girls and laundry workers who accompanied the gold rush. The Canadian male never entirely outgrew this notion that sex was an activity for days when it was too cold to shaft a mine.

The exception to this attitude was held by the French-Canadian male, to whom sexual intercourse was a means of continuing the holy war against the English (''the revenge of the cradle''). The birth of the Dionne quintuplets (1934) was the greatest French victory since the capture of Schenectady. It inspired the French-Canadian to father very large families, yet the English refused to surrender. Indeed, if anyone was developing dark shadows under his eyes, it was *le Canadien*. What had seemed at first the ideal kind of military skirmish, in terrain where the English needed guides and still failed to make any appreciable advance before freeze-up, proved to be a war of attrition, one whose casualties wanted to be sent anywhere but home.

As a result, the Quebec birth rate dropped. The English-Canadian birth rate dropped less because, at that time, the English method of contraception was the British Square, which held off penetration both front and rear but was useless against people hiding behind trees. By 1970, both the founding races had developed the same mature regard for sex, namely, that it was wiser to take a cold shower.

How, then, did Canada become the sex-mad milieu that, towards the end, attracted Danish and Swedish tourists seeking novelties in perversion?

As with so many other social influences, awareness of sex was imported into Canada from the United States. In the beginning, it came in with industrial calendars, which bore the likeness of semi-nude women in provocative poses, such as washing a Scottie dog. The Scottie became a very popular breed in Canada, with no one really knowing why. Canadians had no idea of the widespread effect of these calendars that were mailed free by manufacturers of plumbing fixtures, lubricants, and similar American products and that found their way into the back shops of thousands of Canadian firms whose front office displayed a calendar from the Bank of Montreal.

These U.S. girlie calendars gave young Canadian men a new and disturbing interest in the passage of time. Youth also associated naked women with mechanical appliances—a dangerous background for experimentation. Renaissance Europe became once again conscious of the human body, as glorified by the Greeks and Romans, but in Canada it happened by courtesy of the Dazey Tool Company of Cicero, Illinois. (This was the *female* human body. So far as is known, Canadians never did become conscious of the male human body.)

Later, the American calendar not only became more daring but was exceeded in pornographic material by U.S. men's magazines, obscene films, smutty novels, and other manifestations of behavior that in Canada would have normally been buried under snow for most months of the year. Worse. most Canadians got their sex education second-hand from American paperbacks, written by psychiatrists and doctors telling them everything they had always wanted to know about sex but were too far north to ask.

Canadians were flummoxed at being told that there was more than one way of making love. They thought that an alternate positon meant working at a desk. They felt that it was bad enough being under the shop foreman all day without doing it for recreation. The one area of life where the Canadian could hope to find simplicity, the direct approach, became a frightening jungle of Latin words: fellatio, cunnilingus, coitus interruptus, et cetera (et cetera put the wind straight up him).

A Canadian football player who was handed a sweater with the number 69 didn't know whether he was on the special team or was simply the back-up to the coach's wife. The Canadian logger, emerging from the bush in search of the kind of fun that was basic to the country's primary industry, strayed into the sex boutique and developed doubts about the virtuosity of his performance. In severe cases, the forester was unable to plant a seedling without foreplay.

Another major blow to conventional sex in Canada was the surfeit of blue films that accompanied the introduction of pay TV. Couples watched the feats of sexual athletes projected on their bedroom ceiling and were at first titillated but later intimidated, finally lapsing into an induced impotence.

Too late, people realized that the secret of the popularity of sex over the ages was the general ignorance about it and, above all, the absence of a basis of comparison. When Canadians became fully exposed to the sexual phantasies of Swedes, Frenchmen, Britons, and other more mature nations, what became aroused was their inferiority complex. They distrusted their own attempts to make dirty films as second-rate and, because Canadian film makers had to depend on government financing, they could not explore obscene acts that had not already been approved by parliament.

While the rude masculinity of Canadian society was being eroded by foreign notions of sex which created insecurity in both the home and, more important, the motel, another U.S.-born movement was wreaking even greater devastation among Canada's sexual mores: women's liberation. Women's liberation was Eve returning the rib to Adam with instructions on where to implant it.

Canada was particularly susceptible to pandemic feminism because Canadians were a reasonable, rather than an emotional, people, and reason could find no argument against complete equality for women. Worse, Canadian women could think of no good reason for not accepting it. In other countries (France and Italy, for example) the roles of the sexes were so well and pleasurably defined that women were able to use the same public lavatory as men without claiming it as a victory for the clitoral orgasm. Most Canadians did not know a clitoral orgasm from a hay baler, but their rationalism dictated the right of every woman to have one, though it meant that her husband had to move his dinghy out of the carport.

Louise Riel and Her/His Rebellion

In the midst of this general acceptance in Canada of women's rights, there rose a renegade who saw equality as a loss of privilege—Louise Riel.

Some called her mad. Others said that she had a skin problem that made it easier to wear a dress. Whatever her mental state, we do know that Louise Riel first came to public notice in Manitoba, where she led an attack on a group of women who were picketing the Miss Blue Bomber beauty contest. She burned her jockstrap.

Louise Riel called herself a half-breed. By this she meant that half of her wanted to breed, the other half didn't, and both halves changed places a lot. Her life was made miserable by Manitobans who heard her called the Transsexual and wanted to know if she had a dome car.

Louise Riel then had an operation that changed her sex from male to female. Since the operation cost her a lot of money, she was enraged by the women's liberation movement, which was eliminating the distinction between her photos of Before and After.

Louise Riel had visions of a sexually independent state on the banks of the Red River that would protect the right of women to be regarded as sex objects and to be used in advertising a wide range of products for the home or office. In her wild forays to achieve this goal, she had the support of a motley band of housewives and Tupperware salesmen.

She seized a Hudson's Bay Company pantsuit department, storming the escalator while wearing nothing but a front-opening bra and with even less support from her artillery. She took as prisoners several mannequins wearing jeans, but these later proved to be men and had to be released. A store detective was slightly wounded in the melee when a lesbian novel, hurled by one of Riel's followers, shattered an anti-shoplifting mirror and severed his paging unit.

As a result of this episode, the federal government declared Louise Riel to be an outlaw, and ordered that she be arrested on sight and forced to remove her false eyelashes. Riel responded defiantly by taking refuge in the north woods, where she set up a secret plant to manufacture bustles, a Victorian article of feminine apparel designed to accentuate the bottom and help middle-aged men to distinguish girls from boys.

"We attack from the rear!"—Louise Riel's celebrated *cri de guerre*—won her the unexpressed respect of a considerable number of Canadian men whose sex life had been narrowed down to taking hormone shots. Emboldened by her

132

success against sexually egalitarian authority, she captured a warehouse in which a group of Status of Women extremists had stored a quantity of powder—after-shave powder. For several days, both sides exchanged epithets broadcast over portable loudspeakers (The Battle of the Little Bullhorn), Louise Riel showing a marked superiority in the deployment of four-letter words, till the feminists called up reserves from the Campfire Girls.

To escape prosecution, Louise Riel moved to Montana, posing as an Avon lady. During this time she was elected to parliament twice, without attending, thereby winning a permanent place in the hearts of Canadians.

She was brought out of retirement by the promoters of the Miss Canada contest, who needed help in providing credibility for the winner. For many years, Canada had been choosing a Miss Canada to compete in various international beauty contests, which Miss Canada never won, failing even to reach the finals. In 1996, Miss Canada was the subject of controversy over whether she should have been entered in the Miss Universe contest or the Mr. Universe contest.

The promoters of the Miss Canada contest were, therefore, under militant pressure from feminists to abandon the struggle and use the money to improve loan facilities at the Sperm Bank. (It was not till after the turn of the century that the Sperm Bank became one of Canada's chartered banks, with headquarters in Niagara Falls. The First Canadian Sperm Bank was notable for its personable male tellers, one of whom was featured in its advertising—"Hi, I'm Marty. . . .")

In what was to be the last stand of "the female stereotype"—as it was called by the feminists—Louise Riel gathered together a group of male voyeurs and led them to Regina's Wascana Park, where she removed all her clothes, stood on a fountain, and declared herself officially open. Refusing to descend, she was devoured by black flies. Louise Riel was later venerated by Canadians as something of a martyr, though her sanity was never definitely established.

Another factor upsetting the historical manliness of Canada was the Gay Liberation Movement. The gays were male homosexuals, but this was not as repellent to Canadians as the suggestion of gaiety. They viewed light-heartedness as an unnatural act. It affronted most Canadians to think that persons of the same sex—consenting adults or otherwise—should engage in a relationship outside the normal bounds of apathy.

This feeling against the Gay Liberation Movement may or may not have in-

fluenced Canadians to give up standing for "God Save the Queen" (or if they did stand, they stood with their backs to the wall). Nevertheless, the gays became a politically significant minority group, especially so after the election to power of the New Democratic Party, which had adopted bisexualism as a party plank. Pledged to make Canada completely bisexual, the government began with the civil servants. The retraining of government employees to enable them to engage in intercourse in both official sexes encountered a good deal of resistance, though not as much as the program to teach them French.

As might be expected, these changing sex roles resulted in the mass withdrawal known as the Greening of Canada. People found a more reliable companionship in plants. Beginning in the 1970s, Canadians, and especially Canadian women, turned to the house plant for affection. Shops selling potted flora sprang up in urban areas like weeds to cater to the fierce demand for what one Canadian poet called "a frond I can trust."

It was believed that the house plant responded to a display of love. Since it did so without talking and with little possibility of its walking out on a person, it made the ideal room-mate (or so it was believed). The first hint of serious problems for the herbophile came when a husband in Halifax sued his wife for divorce and named a rubber plant as corespondent. A Toronto housewife caught her husband taking a shower with her philodendron and shot both. And after a window cleaner who had moved in with a young widow was strangled to death by her jealous grape ivy, the country was stunned by the jury verdict of not guilty because of temporary insanity.

These deviations from the simple Canadian method of increasing the population (by immigration) culminated in the total loss of sexual identity. Both men and women were unsure which they were, and this uncertainty killed square dancing. In all but a few remote areas that sex education had not reached, Canadians became the only people whose mating season was cancelled if it rained.

Sex

Conceptual Art

9/The Rape of the Locker Room

During the nineteenth century, Canada found a sex surrogate in rough, contact sports played by teams of males who recognized these games as a safer way of becoming exhausted, even though the contact resulted in a skull fracture.

Lacrosse, Canadian football, English rugby, and particularly the national game, ice hockey, combined the physical impact of love-making with the cathartic violence of war. One reason why Canada was such a peace-loving country, internationally, was that she was so bloody-minded in the arena. To Canadians, Genghis Khan was a sissy because he wore a helmet.

From a study of photos of Canadian athletes during the heyday of competitive sports in that country, it is clear that a gap in the front teeth was the proof of having attained manhood. The only parallel in folk custom was that of the Wonghi tribe of New South Wales, in which youths approaching manhood were initiated at a secret ceremony that none but men were allowed to witness. Part of the ritual consisted of knocking out a tooth and giving a new name to the novice to indicate the change from youth to manhood. While the tooth was being knocked out, an instrument known as a bull-roarer—a piece of wood

140

with serrated edges—was whirled around rapidly in the air to create a loud humming sound.

In the Canadian ritual, the bull-roarer was replaced by an organ playing "Hold That Tiger." The novice was given a new name (Bobby), unless his name was Jesus, in which case he was sent down to an American minor league. With his incisors knocked out, the novice had the caved-in profile of an old man. Canadians were thus the only North American tribe to have instant elders.

However, the stabilizing effect of dentally extractive sport on Canadian society was compromised with the introduction of paying spectators, who placed more emphasis on the home team's winning than on the unaffected joy of maiming an opponent. In order to win, Canadian teams imported players from other countries—football players from the United States, soccer players from Britain, baseball players from Puerto Rico, hockey players from Sweden, and—being without shame—ping-pong players from Taiwan.

The professional football players from the United States were mostly black men who had been found unworthy of the National Football League. The Canadian Football League became a refuge for blacks fleeing the slavery of being chained to the bench by American coaches. The Canadian public adjusted to the fact that the Canadian football hero was an Afro-American desperate enough to try to carry a ball across the ice of Taylor Field in Regina while pursued by a baying pack of also-rans.

This Canadianization of *Uncle Tom's Cabin* had, as its climactic scene, what was called Grey Cup Day. Like the Roman Saturnalia, Grey Cup was a winter-time orgy by which the people reassured themselves of their chances of surviving till spring. The Grey Cup game was held in a different city each year in order to give the previous city time to recover. In 1993, the football game was eliminated from the proceedings because it interrupted the less structured custom of dismantling the local hotels. By the turn of the century, most Canadians had forgotten the original reason for Grey Cup Day—like Christmas— except for the parents who attended school concerts in which their children played the part of angels heralding the arrival of a very high punt.

The metamorphosis of spectator sport in Canada was hastened by the successful insistence of women to play on teams with men, thanks to which the kissing and hugging after scoring a goal tended to overshadow the rest of the play. The player who showed desire was thrown out of the game. He could also be thrown out for not showing desire. For many coaches of mixed teams of men and women, the game plan consisted of not showing up.

Once participation had been recognized by schools and colleges as more important than competitiveness, it was inevitable that the CFL Lineman of the Year award would be won by a two hundred fifty pound grandmother. She was chosen because she had great hands, tickling the opposing lineman till he was helpless. With girls on a football team, the game held the spectators' interest only till they broke the huddle. The public looked for new stars in Canadian spectator sports and found them in the players' agents and lawyers.

The Dotted Line Backer

Eagle Alanson was the first superstar among the lawyers contending for contracts in professional sport. Other legal representatives of athletes specialized in one sport, but Eagle not only negotiated equally well for left winger or right winger, he was undisputed champion of the contractual pentathlon: ice hockey, football, tennis, soccer, and curling (which he revolutionized by playing both ends against the middle).

The athlete's agent had to be equally at home on artificial ice and artificial turf, yet had to keep his poise if he put his foot on something real.

The Sports Hall of Fame, Nairobi, has preserved—along with his ball-point pen—the tape recording of an interview granted by Eagle Alanson after he had retired from professional sport, at the age of eighty-four, to devote himself entirely to the practice of law. An extract:

142

Q: Eagle, what was your greatest triumph as the hockey players' all-star agent?

A: When we beat the Russians.

Q: What was the score?

A: Two point eight million to thirty-two.

Q: That is two point eight million *dollars*.

A: There's any other kind?

Q: What was the thirty-two dollars?

A: We gave each of the Russian hockey players a buck Mickey Mouse watch. Our guys got a piece of the television rights. What I call poetry in motion.

Q: The contract for that Team Canada series was treasured as a classic of hockey gamesmanship.

A: I got a lot of help from my team.

Q: That would be Alanson, Alanson, Alanson, Alanson, and Hepchick.

A: You left out one Alanson.

Q: Sorry. In your judgment, sir, at what point did Canadian spectator sport lose its popular appeal, so that today the seventy thousand seat Montreal Olympic Stadium is used to graze cattle?

A: The decline began when the Canadian professional athlete's legal representative lost his stamina.

Q: You have always been a strong advocate of conditioning for the player's agent.

A: When I stepped into that smoke-filled room against the tough club owners and media executives, I had to be ready. The game was won in the corners, you know. Too many kids came out of law school thinking that all they had to do was suit up and take a few practice shots with their notary stamp.

Q: The agent had to have all the moves.

A: Second effort—that's what won players' strikes. The determination to cancel a whole season, if necessary, to preserve a winning record at the bargaining table. Without it, the players have no idea why they are knocking each other down. Which is what killed professional sport in this country.

For a brief period, violent games in Canada were replaced by tennis and squash. After so many years of ice hockey, however, Canadians were unable to adapt to a game that was won by putting shots over the net instead of into it. No Canadian tennis player was invited to partake of the strawberries and cream of Wimbledon, let alone the Byzantine splendour of Caesar's Palace in Las Vegas. The only Canadian tennis player of note, Raoul Nill, who won the Tibetan Open of 1998, was forced to retire from the game in disgrace when it was discovered that he was using steroids to build up his hair. He combed his hair over his face so that his opponent couldn't tell whether he was running backwards or forwards.

Because of the difficulty in reserving a court, however, both tennis and squash were associated with the upper class. The business executive who arrived at the office carrying a squash racket was deferred to as a Brahmin, whereas the untouchables carried bowling balls. Of all these Canadian sports only one—golf—has survived with today's neo-Neanderthal, who has a natural rapport with mercilessly clubbing something smaller than himself.

Sports

The Blubber Set

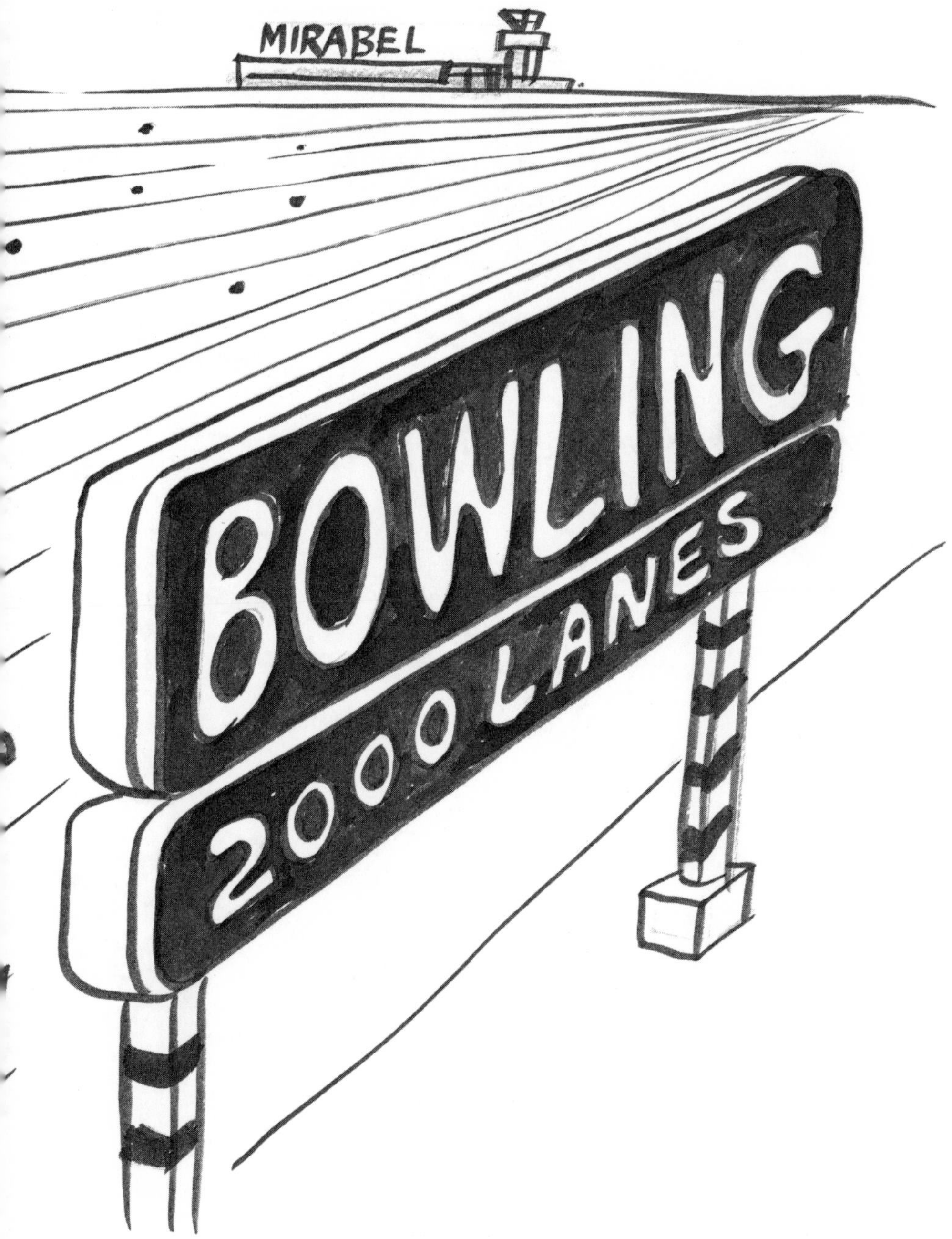
MIRABEL
BOWLING
2000 LANES

10/Belly Worship Rampant

Civilizations have overcome indulgence in gladiatorial games, licentiousness, and sexual perversion, but none has come back from the two-hour lunch. For Canada, the years of prosperity and growth coincided with a simple, not to say stark, attitude towards food. Canadians believed that God would provide, and, as a result, some were thirty-five years old before they were weaned.

In line with eating to live rather than living to eat, the early Canadian meal had two courses: the first helping, and the second helping. Taking a third helping was considered to be an affectation.

Diet was conservative. The Puritan Fathers of the United States were able to thank the Indian for introduction to the turkey and to popcorn, but the early settlers of Canada learned nothing from the natives except to eat where truck drivers ate. The Canadian pioneer created the virtue of the home-cooked meal, served to a large family and the hired hands in the kitchen, where the smell of home-baked bread was so strong a man's nose rose overnight. The Canadian restaurant was thought of as part of the price one paid for being a travelling salesman.

When a Canadian was forced to "eat out" in the early days, because of a mishap such as his wife's passing away, he was scrupulous to choose a restaurant that graced its window with the sign, All White Help. Canadians had a kind of religious phobia—a taboo—about food cooked or served by hands other than pale enough to be loved beside the Shalimar. They believed that a meal touched by a non-white jeopardized their virility and brought on wheat rust.

Since nearly all restaurant meals in Canada up to 1950 were prepared by Chinese cooks, it was necessary to partition off the kitchen area in order to preserve the illusion of racial purity. The higher-class restaurant hired a string ensemble to muffle the outbursts of Oriental profanity beyond the pale. The Chinese cooks did not prepare Chinese food, which was considered to be unfit for human consumption, but turned out solidly Anglo-Saxon meals which reassured the patron by not tasting of anything.

The procedure in eating a Canadian restaurant meal was for the patron to take a small mouthful of the food to confirm that it was bland and, therefore, safe to eat. He then picked up a bottle of a sauce called Ketchup. Ketchup was essential to the early Canadian restaurant meal; no one would think of eating without it, any more than he would leave uncovered his mother's grave.

When the food was completely submerged in Ketchup, it was eaten as quickly as possible and with the eyes closed to avoid seeing an ingredient with which the diner was not familiar. Although the Canadian diner rarely finished the meal, he did not ask for a doggie bag, apparently because he loved animals. He then left the restaurant, taking a handful of toothpicks and holding one between his lips to show that he had not compromised his contempt for the establishment. Thus the early Canadian restaurant took little time from the patron's work day and helped to strengthen respect for the Canadian home as a vital extension of the stomach.

It is difficult to set an exact date for the loss of gastronomic innocence among Canadians, though it seems to fall somewhere between the raj of the drive-in and the first forays by the Galloping Gourmet. In much the same way that Marco Polo introduced Europeans to the spices and exotic fruits of the Far East, so did the Canadian troops of World War II bring home from France and Italy word of strange, gustatory delights called pizza . . . coq-au-vin . . . Chelsea bun. . . . Curiosity begetting hedonism, Canadian restaurants began to serve food in the "Continental" style, meaning that the patron felt guilty about asking the waiter for Ketchup and fetched it himself.

At first Canadians were so ashamed of enjoying food in public that they insisted that the lighting be removed from the restaurant. The diner was placed, usually against his better judgment, at a table on which sat a candle. He then concealed himself inside the cavernous menu while the waiter lit the candle. Some, more shy than others, ate the whole meal without emerging from the *carte des vins*. Others who dined out more regularly developed a nocturnal sensory system: vestigial eyes, whiskers, and the bat's sonar capability to find its way in the dark by bouncing short sound waves off the maitre d'. Nevertheless, many died, put to the sword when they stumbled too close to a waiter preparing a flaming shish kebab. Families that included small children roped themselves together, in this dark age of the Canadian restaurant, but still had to walk across burning coals to reach their New York steak.

During the 1970s, Canadians became bold enough to re-introduce illumination in restaurants and saw for the first time what they had been eating. Lamentably, instead of recoiling from the sight of fondue and raw fish and wantonly wild rice, they became fascinated by these extraterritorial dishes and succumbed to cuisine that made a mockery of the virtues nurtured by the sainted trinity: Meat and Two Veg.

158

The Garlic Catastrophe

Toronto was the scene of the worst of these excesses. Montreal, the older city whose French population had preserved a working relationship with flavour, did not yield so immoderately to the restaurant craze as did the once-staid ''city of churches,'' where almost overnight seekers of salvation turned from the Archbishop of Canterbury to the Bicarbonate of Soda.

Although they could not afford to gluttonize in as wide a variety of ethnic restaurants as were found in Toronto, the inhabitants of Vancouver were more sorely afflicted because the two-hour lunch slowed down a pace of life that was already sluggish to the point of inertia. They flocked to restaurants night after night, and on the Sabbath, to eat things that they formerly treated with slug bait. Vancouver businessmen languidly winkled escargots from their shells and dreamed of owning their own mobile homes.

But most of all, Vancouver became fatally enamoured of garlic.

No one knows how Canada discovered garlic. It may, like the French kiss, have been accidentally brought over from Europe, a garlic bud lying undetected among a returning batch of Canadian entries in the Cannes Film Festival. It is certain, however, that garlic swiftly took over the restaurant roll—the one part of the meal that Canadians trusted. Garlic bread became the icon of good eating in Canada. Every restaurant with any pretension to class placed the sacramental basket on the table, and Canadians ate of the bread in the belief that it was an act of communion with the sophisticated. Heresy was dealt with severely. The diner who produced a medical certificate signed by his physician, stating that the diner was allergic to members of the onion family, might escape with no more than having his table moved into the back alley. But in 1979, a visitor to Vancouver from Paris who asked the waiter for plain French bread with his dinner was summarily executed by a party of B.C. truck loggers who surrounded him and exhaled.

The Garlic Catastrophe in Vancouver was caused by a freak combination of circumstances: atmospheric inversion, the technological problem of air conditioning, and a day when ninety per cent of the people lunching on expense accounts breathed out at the same time. The disaster was not unforeseen. Municipal engineers had pointed out that the air pumps used to expel the garlic-laden fumes from hundreds of restaurants were dangerously over-extended, coughing bolts, and falling off roofs. As early as 1974, Vancouver residents had complained of the ferocious odour roaming the downtown streets, but it was not till a hot, humid, windless day of July, 1989, that the deadly miasma reached critical mass. A salami-and-mushroom-shaped cloud formed over the city. Dozens of people were trampled to death trying to escape the garlic gas by pushing their way into restaurants, while others tried to flee to the countryside and collided with those running towards the scene to satisfy their morbid interest.

The Vancouver city fathers responded to the Garlic Catastrophe by banning air conditioning in restaurants. Garlic continued to extend its terrible dominion over the populace. In this, it was abetted by the manufacturers of breath mints, who imported garlic buds in vast quantities for free distribution to Canadian chefs. There is, therefore, no need to consider as apocryphal the story that a Vancouver bon vivant met a skunk in Stanley Park, and it was the skunk that waved the white flag.

During this reign of terror, home cooking lost all remnants of prestige. With both parents working, quickness and ease of preparation were the first essentials in the home kitchen, with the microwave oven enjoying a brief period of popularity till it was found that the microwaves changed the molecular structure of food in such a way that after a few years the user turned into a dwarf.

160

As more Canadian men took over the home preparation of meals, they tried to retain something of their masculinity by performing an elaborate, outdoor ceremony called a ''cook-out,'' in their backyard, which was thereby made uninhabitable. The cook wore a funny apron and an overblown chef's hat to reassure neighbors that he was not immolating himself for reasons to be taken seriously. The cook seared the flesh of an animal over smouldering charcoal, while his guests drank heavily and ventured opinions as to why the choking clouds of smoke had not discouraged the equally thick clouds of insects attracted by the cremation. The cook-out was banned after the Great Fire of Calgary.

The patio barbecue had, however, accustomed Canadians to taking alcohol with their meals, regardless of the condition of the food. Even the TV dinner—a frozen preparation consumed while watching television, as a supreme test of endurance—was accompanied by fine French wines, though always against their will.

TIMBER!

In its earlier days, Canada had believed in the separation of both church and state, and food and drink. Canadians drank to get drunk. They did not confuse their stomach by introducing extraneous matter other than the chaser. They were also careful not to drink in front of the children, because it was easy to fall over them.

Effete drinking habits, such as using a corkscrew instead of breaking the top off the bottle, were brought back from Europe by Canadian tourists. The hardy rules of the saloon and the beer parlor were corrupted by lounges that served cocktails, foreign concoctions that distracted the bartender from his primary purpose of helping the drinker find his mouth.

Heroic Canadian spirits such as Navy rum and Calgary Red Eye were subjected to the debilitating influence of fruit juice. In their effort to look worldly to their companions, people ordered depraved mixtures: the Bloody Mary, the Bloody Caesar (vodka with clam juice), the Virgin Caesar (vodka sucked through a straw). Flunkies were publicly berated for bringing a drink with a twist of lemon instead of lime. Grown men sniffed corks, sometimes bunging a nostril in their rapture.

Canadian wine, also known as the Wrath of Grapes, was spurned as beneath contempt by the cognoscenti. Because of the variety of grape grown in Canada, the mash had the robust flavor of Firestone retread. The wine was therefore served only at semi-social functions (the ''wine-and-cheese party''), where the host sought to ensure that the next meeting would be held at someone else's house.

The thirst for imported wines impaired Canada's balance of trade, which was already feeling pretty giddy. But this did not deter the people from mob scenes in the liquor store, where they filled their shopping carts and became involved in alcohol-related accidents before they even reached the check-out. The Dionysian frenzy reached a peak in a West Vancouver wine specialty store when the assistant manager was shredded by flying glass after two matrons simultaneously reached for the last bottle of Gamza.

162

From toasting the Queen with a glass of water, Canadians moved very rapidly to toasting anybody, with a different wine for each course, followed by a liqueur with the coffee, and an after-dinner mint julep. Unlike the European, however, the crapulous Canadian never learned to devote most of the evening to the meal of many wines, instead trying to combine it with a Parent-Teachers Association meeting. The result was a swift decline in the quality of P.T.A. meetings, the parents and teachers setting fire to those schools not already destroyed by the students. For the same reason, at evening bowling leagues more legs were taken off by balls than in the Battle of Trafalgar.

By the time Canadians had learned to spend more time over their liquid lunch and dinner, imported wines were cut off by loss of transportation in the energy crisis, and people now spent three hours over their meal without knowing why. New uses were found for the wine bucket, if it was not too tall to go under the bed. The back alleys of Canadian cities were littered with the forms of ex-wine stewards who had sought oblivion in cough syrup. Canada lost her cellar before she had time to turn the bottles.

Chronology of the Spread of Hedonism in Newfoundland

1950   Building of railway across Newfoundland

1963   Addition of trains to the Newfoundland railway

1968   Royal commission of enquiry into problems of the Newfoundland railway

1970   Purchase of a locomotive to pull trains along the Newfoundland railway

1977   Publication, by a St. John's publisher, of the book *100 Other Things To Do In a Dense Fog*

1978   Newfoundlanders self-conscious about eating off continental shelf. Introduction of chairs in restaurants

1980   Spread of acupuncture to Newfoundland, resulting in deaths of millions of Chinese

1984   Bloody raids upon one another by Newfoundland villagers, plundering for resin for their fiddles

1985   CBC studios in Newfoundland destroyed by internecine war between mixed choirs of Hymn Singers.

2000   Island paradise engulfed by wave of Hollandaise sauce

Food

Candlelight Dinner

Beach Party

11/The Lamp of Learning Unplugged

From the earliest days, Canadians respected the ability to read and write and do sums, because this was the only way to keep ahead of the Indians when counting their furs. The oldest Canadian literary form was the ledger. Much emphasis was placed on penmanship, because the numbers and letters had to survive the long crossing to the chief accountant of the Hudson's Bay Company in London.

Discipline, too, was stressed. In this respect, Canada's school system was modeled on that of Mother England, except that the pupils were flogged with native woods—Ontario birch, prairie willow, western maple. Canadians had the same policy with the pupil as with the Ketchup bottle: if you beat it hard enough on the bottom, sooner or later something will happen above the neck.

The immediate applicator of this philosophy was the pioneer school teacher, usually female, who did not wait for the pupil to do something wrong but thrashed him while he was still small enough for her to be able to handle him. This was called Primary Education.

Because the typical Canadian school had only one room and one teacher, the same subjects were taught to all grades, and graduation was determined by the student's being too big to get his knees under the desk. This practice persisted till well into the twenty-first century. It was called Secondary Education. The main difference between the Grade One student and the Grade Twelve student was that when the Grade Twelve student asked the teacher to accompany him to the washroom, it was as a hostage.

During the mid-twentieth century, Canadian schooling became imbued with the principles of permissive education, which had previously been tried in other parts of the world, but never where the children had access to chain saws. No one seems to know for sure how permissive education got into the Canadian classroom, one theory being that it slipped in through the window of the Staff Room while the teachers were busy rolling funny cigarettes. Instead of stressing the skills of preparing a neat statement of accounts receivable, permissive schooling attempted to treat the child as a human being—a mistake that was not discovered till too late.

In place of penmanship, the teacher gave instruction in what was variously called Guidance, Personal Development, Effective Living, or Dirty Recess. This course was expanded to include sex education, one of the factors responsible for the loss of interest in normal sexual intercourse in Canada. Once fornication became academic, the libido turned to other devices such as the electric vibrator, the French horn, and of course, avilingus, or oral stimulation of the budgie.

This would not have been so serious had not older people believed that the young were doing the only thing they knew how to spell.

Parents were also alarmed by new math, as a supplement to sex education, because one plus one was replaced by groups of ten. Actually, new math was an attempt to make students understand the system of calculation used by computers, which Canadians had found to be a useful tool for freeing the brain for premature senility. They later found that they were mathematically helpless if their batteries went dead, a crisis situation dramatically demonstrated when the giant computer of the University of Alberta broke down, and the entire department of mathematics had to be taken away in restraining jackets after the professors tried to total their class attendance by counting on their fingers.

These flaws in permissive education led to a return to the ''basics'' and ''the three Rs,'' to the era of sex training known as the Restoration of the Grope. Many teachers were unable to make the adjustment to the classroom as a place of learning. They fled in terror from a swarm of spelling bees. As graduates of the permissive generation that believed that it was seemly for a man to cry, school principals who now had to give a pupil the strap burst into tears. They cringed before the new, structured parent who demanded that the student caught chewing gum have his jaw wired shut till the next report card.

In every province of Canada, the teachers' federations revolted against the return of hard work in the classroom as reactionary. In 1986, the Saskatchewan teachers marched on the capital, angrily beating their chalk erasers to protest

the phasing out of the Free Period as a compulsory subject. In Victoria, the minister of education was stabbed with leatherwork picks on the steps of the legislature by a group of B.C.T.F. conspirators fearing Latin.

These disturbances grew into pitched battles fought between teachers and parents in violent reaction to the teachers' campaign to purge the school system of students. From about 1950 on, the teachers had been gradually reducing their involvement in the classroom, where they were exposed to what they recognized to be the most objectionable part of the educational process, namely, the student. By increasing the proportion of "professional days," "teacher study sessions," "semester breaks," "student survival field trips," and other exercises in teacher absence, the teachers by the late eighties were able to issue a manifesto stating that the reduced number of hours of contact with the students did not justify enrollment.

172

The Abolition of Students From Canadian Schools

Eliminating students from the educational system began in the universities, which had been working on the project, in terms of practical research, for many years. One of the fathers of the project, sociology professor Dr. Elf Moonglow, blamed skimpy government grants for slowing the research that was to emancipate the academic from the drudgery of instruction.

The professorial sabbatical had provided the first breakthrough in identifying the extraneousness of the student. By 1960, it was generally accepted that the professor who had to teach a class was a failure. The more enterprising faculty members met their students only long enough to direct them to the "lab"—chemistry lab, French lab, comparative religions lab—where the student was stored among audio-visual aids till the milder weather of spring made it possible to transplant him into an outdoor seminar. Other experiments, however, that discouraged mice and monkeys from attending university, failed to deter human beings. To remove the expendable element, it was necessary to raise the student fees to such a high level that the bursar had to work behind a lead shield.

Most universities retained at least one student, for the sake of appearances, but Simon Fraser University, in Burnaby, British Columbia, fulfilled the dream of becoming totally student-free. Scholars came from all parts of the world to admire the serenity of the magnificent campus, where only the football team was allowed to tiptoe to the stadium on Saturday afternoons, when the offices were closed.

The attempt by public schools to duplicate this ideal atmosphere for scholarship was strenuously resisted by Canadian working mothers, who needed the classroom as a supervised area in which to park their children during the gainful hours of the day. The first open clash between the two forces occurred on March 11, 1990, when the teachers of the Isaac Brock Secondary School of Windsor, Ontario, en route to a six-week staff study session at the Detroit Motel and Body Rub, were ambushed at the Pauline Johnson Bridge by a raiding party of Single Mothers, with heavy losses on both sides. The provincial governments hastily passed legislation requiring teachers to show up for classes unless they had a note from their analyst, but they were too late. Ninety per cent of the schools had been totally destroyed by vandalism and Meet The Teachers Night.

The remaining schools were taken over by African missionaries, black people who accepted a good deal of hardship in order to come to Canada and teach

173

Canadian children the rudiments of literacy, combined with religious instruction in fetish worship, particularly that of the phallus. This explains how, by the turn of the century, the Peace Tower of the parliament buildings in Ottawa had become the penile totem before which thousands of young Canadians gathered at Easter to sacrifice a goat.

Canadians had been prepared for instruction in devil worship by films shown in cinemas and on television during the 1970s, frightening scenes that accompanied the devouring of the popcorn-spirit. Demonism filled the vacuum created by loss of faith in the Liberal party.

Yet Canada began her story as a devoutly Christian nation, satisfied that Satan would not seek her souls unless Hell froze over. Canadians had a choice of High Church—Roman Catholic or Anglican—and those that couldn't stand heights became Methodists. They strictly observed the Sabbath as a day of rest, insisting that everyone must rest as much as everyone else, because the wages of sin were bad enough without paying time and a half.

But the Lord led them into green pastures, called golf courses, and by the middle of the twentieth century Canadians had added a new name for divinity: Bingo. The devotion with which they attended communion with Bingo exceeded all earlier forms of mass. Belial, Beelzebub, and Bingo—but of these only Bingo battened on betting on two cards at once.

Another departure from the rational was the emergence, during the 1950s, of a quasi-religious movement called the Counter-culture—so called because its adherents sustained themselves by shoplifting goods from counters. The initiates sought to establish the brotherhood of man, which was found to be incompatible with doing homework. They sat in a circle, cross-legged, passing around the pipe of peace and experiencing a sensory exaltation that transcended earning a living.

These young people also wore odd garments made of material they could believe in: leather, wrought iron, uncarded wool from sheep that had eaten nothing but wild rice. They were called "hippies" (a name whose derivation is obscure, but may have come from the Greek *hippo,* or horse, since the men wore their hair in a pony tail).

Highly nomadic, the youthful hippies roamed Canada from sea to sea, weather permitting. They proved that it is not easy to get an education, even for those that have dropped out of school. They established communication with the Ineffable, but it turned out to be a party line.

174

The major effect of the hippies, however, was to draw attention to the environment, which Canadians had previously thought of as being the responsibility of the city sanitation department. They did this by using the female hemp plant, which when smoked produced a kind of euphoria without the litter of beer cans or herbicide in the short hairs. The environment was sacred to the Canadian hippie, who saw God as a whale. When He wasn't a whale (during the off season), God was a vacant lot. Because of the Canadian's long-standing affinity with the inanimate, it was not hard for the hippie to infuse the general population with the urge to throw oneself in front of a bulldozer. This fanaticism to save a tree, in a nation known to have had other places to urinate, is without parallel.

The only construction that was blessed in the hippies' sight was that of the sewage treatment plant. Of the three holy orders of sewage plant—Primary, Secondary, and Tertiary—the Tertiary was the basilica of the new faith. The power to turn urban effluent into organic fertilizer was revered by both the Mennonite and the Milorganite. Organic pilgrims made the hegira each summer to Vancouver, the Canadian city whose mountains offered the biggest challenge to the macrobiotic Mahomet. They built rude shelters on the beaches, where they ate nuts, made love, and played the unleavened guitar.

These "flower people" went to seed in the 1970s, but their influence continued to be felt in a Canada that now had doubts about Growth as benign. Some wanted to have the Growth removed, others wanted to wait to see if it would go away by itself if they ate fewer potato chips. Canadians became uncertain whether progress was represented by using farmland to build another supermarket, or by demolishing a supermarket to plant a park.

For many, the incarnation of the fiend shifted from the Devil to the Developer, for whom the parting of body and soul was just another subdivision. The Canadian found Good and Evil increasingly difficult to identify, even when souvenir programs were sold in the lobby. At times, he became desperate enough to go to his clergyman to distinguish right from wrong, but the clergyman was unwilling to answer till he got the current issue of *Reader's Digest*.

Canadians also questioned the morality of work, which was sometimes involved in having a job. The catechism repeated most piously by Canadians at work was "Thank God it's Friday." ("Thank God it's Thursday"—part of the litany of the four-day work week—dates from the religious dissension over moving the Sabbath to Monday in order to make a longer weekend.)

176

These changes show that the Canadian was less concerned about where his soul was going than about where his body had been. He had a holy terror of bad breath and body odour, which were to him the fundamentals of reality ("I stink, therefore I am"). He visualized God as something that gave twenty-four hour protection, eternity available as either a spray or roll-on. Right to the end, Canadians continued to chew breath mints—the Immaculate Confection—and powder their bodies with potions that promised to stopper the sweat glands, a cosmetic exorcism unmatched since the ancient Britons smeared themselves with blue woad to check unsightly Romans.

In this distracted state of mind, they were ready converts to the supernatural beliefs of the native people. On the west coast the first totem pole created entirely by the white man was erected in an auto junk yard, the Thunderbird topping a column made up of the Beetle, the Pinto, the Rabbit, and other symbolic clunks.

Most Canadian churchmen adapted without demur to wearing the shaman's mask and necklace of killer whale teeth, but their prestige never fully recovered from the Pope's refusal to participate in an ecumenical prairie chicken dance.

Education

Graduating Class of '98 in Remedial Reading

*Winner of the Golden Beer Can Award in recognition
of twenty-two continuous years on the UIC circuit*

12/When They Dance the Mediocre

Some are born great, some achieve greatness, some have greatness thrust upon them, and some remained in Canada.

This condition was nowhere more apparent than in the arts. It is sometimes forgotten, in the excitement of excavating their garbage dumps, that Canadians were interested in the arts if there was nothing else much happening. From the earliest times, nearly every Canadian town had an opera house, because the hotel was too noisy for sleep. People who went to the opera house were exposed, sooner or later, to an opera, and this conditioned them to think of culture as something that left town right after the performance. Since most of the operas they went to were sung in Italian or German, Canadians believed that they were being culturally enriched only when they couldn't understand the language. This criterion held long after the visiting European opera companies were replaced by visiting U.S. rock groups. In the arts, Canadians had a firm tradition of finding the sublime in the unintelligible.

They were much less comfortable with Canadian talent, hoping that if they paid no attention to it, it would go away. They had heard that genius was next to madness, but they couldn't imagine an artist crazy enough to stay in Canada. In Canada, nothing distinguished a great Canadian artist so much as the fact that he was living in the United States. If a Canadian artist returned to Canada

(Toronto), he made it clear to the press that it was a brief visit necessitated by the mass burial of his immediate family.

Canadians who remained in the country were encouraged, with government grants and free hospitalization for malnutrition, to become masters of the unexceptional. Anyone who displayed more than a modest competence invited investigation as an illegal immigrant.

In Canadian painting, for example, it was widely assumed that the Group of Seven formed because they were too many to play bridge and not enough for a baseball team.

For many years, Canadian sculpture was limited because Canadians could not think of anyone worth putting on a horse permanently. The dearth of notable Canadian sculptors—compared with the age of Praxiteles—may be attributed to the fact that Canadians were not permitted to exhibit the naked human body in any form without a doctor's prescription. For this reason, most Canadian painters concentrated on faithful reproductions of the anatomy of a barn. The painter who painted the portrait of a Canadian person was assumed to have been someplace where he couldn't find a dead stump.

After the mid-1900s, this naturalistic style was supplemented by murals for the main branches of Canadian chartered banks, paintings called "abstract" because they helped to separate the depositor from his money.

184

Similarly, Canadian poetry celebrated at first the simple features of landscape (one of the few surviving ballads "Will No One Activate My Sludge?" was printed on reconstituted cardboard). More personal verse was acceptable only if the poet was either a paraplegic or Jewish. Poetic expression in Canada was gravely affected by a reduction of the number of railway station men's rooms. For some reason, the lavatories of Canadian Pacific airliners failed to evoke the Muse, substantiating Wordsworth's definition of poetry as "emotion recollected in tranquillity."

By the end of the century, the sole remaining poet in Canada was a computer for which no other employment could be found. The computer, named Fred, ruptured its own circuitry by trying to grow a beard and had to be destroyed.

In prose, Canada was blighted early by an outbreak of humorists. These humorists made Canadians suspicious that all books might possibly contain humour as an additive, which sooner or later could cause the lungs to expel air in the form of a laugh. To be on the safe side, Canadians bought mostly books about historical episodes whose humour content was known to be less than three parts per million. To be doubly safe, they did not read the books themselves but gave them to other Canadians as Christmas presents, the Canadian book symoblizing the Nativity as conception without entertainment.

The So-So Dynasty

In the deserted cities across Canada stand the ruins of strange structures, not beautiful, yet not distinctively ugly: the radio and television studios of the Canadian Broadcasting Corporation.

It was the CBC that organized the various elements of the nondescript in the performing arts—"put it all together," as the phrase was—and, by the minor miracle of electronics, created the Millenium of the Mediocre. (In fact it did not last one thousand years. It just seemed that long.) Never in the history of national culture has mediocrity been elevated to a way of life so triumphantly as it was by this giant government corporation. Competing against the radio and TV networks of Great Britain and the United States, the CBC stoutly avoided the best of both worlds.

The So-So Dynasty—as the CBC is known to students of ancient cultures—was founded during the 1930s, the federal government having decided that because the air belonged to all Canadians, broadcasting should be made as unprofitable as possible.

The first mandarins of the So-So Dynasty were carefully chosen for their patience in developing the kind of radio programs that would make Canadians more receptive to a power failure. As a result, the CBC gradually became the envy of networks in other parts of the world where the popularity of programs was affected by their not being broadcast.

During one brief interval, the CBC threatened to violate its solemn mission, which was the pursuit of excellence so long as it didn't catch it. Fortunately, the corporation was saved from a dangerous precedent by the arrival of a technological marvel that vastly expanded the potential of mediocrity: television. With TV, the So-So Dynasty found inspiration for building much larger temples of nationalized tedium, first in black and white, later in colour. Video-taped recordings of CBC-TV programs in colour have been recovered from the sturdy tombs in which they were placed, along with artifacts that might help them to a better life (from the BBC). These tapes reveal that CBC performers were a florid pink, possibly indicative of chronic embarrassment.

Because it used U.S. programs in most of its prime time, the CBC helped to develop a cadre of highly skilled actors who depended on commercials to stay alive. Canadian actors were equal to any in the world, playing Shakespeare with great finesse, once convinced that Hamlet contained fluoride.

What made the CBC distinctive was that it refused to accept commercials for intimate products associated with personal hygiene. Canadians who watched only the CBC considered women, at a certain time of the month, to be taboo. The bunny ears were removed from the set, and viewers watched National Film Board documentaries of the Arctic Loon.

Despite the massive injection of banality from American television, the So-So Dynasty could not find the money for both its expanding bureaucratic empire and the production of radio and TV programs. The programs were therefore phased out. By the year 2000 A.D., the new CBC broadcasting centres being built in various cities across the country were devoted entirely to closed-circuit television, which was used to monitor the teeming CBC executives and secretarial staff and to ensure that no one used a studio unless the cafeteria was full.

One of the most impressive of these CBC structures is that in the ice of Aklavik, perfectly preserved to this day. Although not one radio or TV program ever emanated from this monumental pile, thousands of CBC employees at one time thronged its ample corridors, carrying to one another's in-baskets memoranda discussing what was the ideal public affairs program for the viewer who was chewing blubber. Today this CBC building is used by the Eskimo as a bordello, one of the few in the world equipped for instant replay.

Alas!
Poor Yorick....

As the So-So Dynasty went into eclipse behind the full moon of its own mediocrity, smaller realms of the arts in Canada were briefly cast into confusion by reports that a Canadian culture had been found. The great Canadian Culture Rush dates from about 1970, with hundreds of Canadian playwrights, painters, musicians, and other artists filing claims. One of the better known claims was that the reason why no Canadian had won a Nobel prize in the arts was that Sweden was jealous of Canadian herring.

The artistic directors of the Stratford (Ontario) Drama Festival refused to deny the find that William Shakespeare was actually born in Canada. The son of a tanner of beaver hides, the playwright moved to England only because of hostile critics among the Iroquois.

In an attempt to popularize Canadian films with the Canadian public, the Canadian Film Development Corporation reclassified films made in Canada as foreign films, but it didn't fool anybody. Nor did it attract visitors from abroad by holding the International Film Festival at a glamorous seaside resort, the Grand Prix de Port Moody never winning the status hoped for it. In fact, the residents of Port Moody failed to show up for the event, though given free passes and the phone numbers of the starlets.

It was also a blow to militant Canadian culturism when the entire company of the National Ballet of Canada defected to Tonga.

On July 1, 1994, to celebrate Canada Day, the country's best-known novelist, Mordecai Dickens Balzac, protested against his publisher's marketing methods by jumping off a fifty-foot-high stack of unsold copies of his mammoth novel, *Now Breaks the Wind*. He did not kill himself, a failing noted in the New York *Times* review of the performance.

The disinclination of Canadian artists to find expression by throwing themselves off a Canadian building was, however, understandable, since Canadian architecture never achieved a distinctive style other than blocking the view. Most buildings conformed to the cereal-box, or headstone, style of architecture which represented an aesthetic vision directed towards total square feet of rentable floor space. The tallest and most prestigious of these structures bore the names of Canada's chartered banks—Toronto-Dominion, Royal Bank, Scotiabank—testifying to the Canadian belief that God's house was easier to approach with a Second Mortgage.

None of these monoliths was ever described as being best seen by moonlight, though one or two in Vancouver inspired admiration when partly obscured by fog.

188

The Arts

Theatre of the Absurd

Art Bank

13/The Super Whooper

Did Canadians originally come from outer space?

Some historians look at the ruins of the Toronto City Hall and say "Yes." The flying saucer is there, almost intact, along with the curved shells that bespeak a race of extraterrestrial beings searching the universe for new sources of concrete. Against this theory must be weighed the more preponderant opinion that colonists from another planet would not have chosen a site so far from a laundromat. The consensus is that Canadians were descended from human beings. The species deteriorated because they were unable to blame their system of government on cholesterol.

Does the disappearance of Canada represent a loss to humanity? Again, the experts are divided in their answer, depending on whether they heard the question. Some point out that Canadians were a mostly inoffensive people who, though they ate few insects, did a fair amount of good in other ways. In them abided faith, hope, and charity (the greatest of these was deductible).

Canadians were not a war-like nation, but engaged in pillage and laying waste only while still young enough to be sent to juvenile court. Their one bloodthirsty activity—clubbing seal pups on the ice—reflected their failure to qualify for the National Hockey League.

Disputing this assessment of Canada as an excusable intermission in the human comedy, other historians say that the country took up too much of the earth's habitable surface for such a low output of the memorable. The Swedes, with a similar population, produced Ingemar Bergman, the Volvo, the smorgasbord, and the nude bathing beach, during the period when the main Canadian accomplishment was Resdan. This was the Unknown Country, unless you had dandruff.

Canada was a country of peace-loving people, but they overdid it. They captured nothing, including the imagination. Whether or not we agree that the planet is better off without Canada, or worse off, or the difference is not measurable, students of civilizations should be curious about the causes of the decline and fall of Canada, in case the same symptoms show up in a people that feels more strongly about becoming extinct.

It has been said—facetiously, one suspects—that Canada chased its identity in ever-diminishing circles till it finally disappeared up its own aspiration. But we must remember that Canada was a product of the Age of Reason. The continuing effort to be reasonable took a lot out of Canadians. They inherited the libertarian principles of the French and American Revolutions, but they never had a revolution they could call their own. They beheaded no one, except in a legal bodycheck. No tea was dumped into Halifax harbor, no dollar thrown across the St. Lawrence.

Because Canadians lacked a Liberty Bell, they were not sure that freedom was all it was cracked up to be. When a Canadian rode through the towns to warn the sleeping inhabitants that the Americans were coming, they turned on the Vacancy sign.

Where an Englishman had said "England expects every man to do his duty," and an American had said "Damn the torpedoes, full speed ahead," a Canadian said "Conscription if necessary, but not necessarily conscription." No nation could survive such a consuming passion for restraint, such a soul-destroying determination that history should judge it clinically sane at the time of suicide.

Can anything be done to save the Canadian as an endangered species? The U.S. National Wild Life Service has expressed guarded optimism. The latest report from its field officers says: "The Canadian Refuge Camper Site in Florida has confirmed arrival of thirty-one families of Canadians to overwinter, as compared with twenty-seven families last year.

"We observe an encouraging sign among these survivors. While it is not yet strong enough to be described as their having any love for one another, they appear to have developed a social cohesion almost equal to that of the Canada goose. If this can be developed further, without the necessity of their laying eggs or travelling in a V formation, we may witness the comeback of the Canadian as a valid form of life."

Postscript . . .

Eric Nicol

Eric Nicol, humorist and dramatist, is Canada's best-loved funny-man. Born in Kingston, Ontario in 1919, he graduated from the University of British Columbia with an M.A. in 1948 and published his first book, *Sense and Nonsense*. Since 1951, Eric Nicol has been a columnist for the Vancouver *Province* and free-lances as well on radio and TV. He married in 1955 and has three children. He has written seven popular stage plays, including *Like Father, Like Fun* and *Beware The Quickly Who*, and has published an impressive list of bestsellers: *The Roving I* (winner of The Leacock Medal for Humour); *Twice Over Lightly; Shall We Join the Ladies?* (Leacock Medal); *Girdle Me a Globe* (Leacock Medal); *In Darkest Domestica; An Uninhibited History of Canada; Say, Uncle; A Herd of Yaks; Russia, Anyone?; Space Age, Go Home!; 100 Years of What?; A Scar is Born; Vancouver; Don't Move!; Still a Nicol; One Man's Media; Letters To My Son; There's A Lot of It Going Around*. With the publication of *Canada Cancelled Because of Lack of Interest*, Nicol maintains his position as **the** *bel esprit* of Canadian letters.

Peter Whalley

Peter Whalley was born in Brockville, Ontario
in 1921 and studied art at the Nova Scotia
College of Art and in Montreal. Since 1948 he
has lived in Morin Heights, Quebec, working as
a free-lance cartoonist for national newspapers
and magazines. Married with three daughters,
he enjoys cross-country skiing and gardening.
Mr. Whalley has been awarded several Art
Director's Awards in Toronto and Montreal,
and, in 1965, he shared first prize in the
International Cartoon Festival. His published
books of drawings include *Man on the Wire;
Broom, Brush and Bucket; Northern Blights;*
and *Phap, The Pornographics of Politics.* He
collaborated with Eric Nicol in *An Uninhibited
History of Canada; Say, Uncle; Russia,
Anyone?;* and *100 Years of What?*